divided by
DEMOCRACY

OTHER LOTUS TITLES

Aitzaz Ahsan	*The Indus Saga: From Pataliputra to Partition*
Alam Srinivas	*Storms in the Sea Wind: Ambani Vs Ambani*
Boman Desai	*A Woman Madly in Love*
Chaman Nahal	*Silent Life: Memoirs of a Writer*
Duff Hart - Davis	*Honorary Tiger: The Life of Billy Arjan Singh*
Frank Simoes	*Frank Unedited*
Frank Simoes	*Frank Simoes' Goa*
Harinder Baweja (ed.)	*Most Wanted: Profiles of Terror*
J.N. Dixit (ed.)	*External Affairs: Cross-Border Relations*
Mallikarjun Mansur Trans. Pt. Rajshekhar Mansur	*Rasa Yatra: My Journey in Music*
M.J. Akbar	*India: The Siege Within*
M.J. Akbar	*Kashmir: Behind the Vale*
M.J. Akbar	*Nehru: The Making of India*
M.J. Akbar	*Riot after Riot*
M.J. Akbar	*The Shade of Swords*
M.J. Akbar	*Byline*
Meghnad Desai	*Nehru's Hero Dilip Kumar: In the Life of India*
Namita Bhandari (ed.)	*India and the World: A Blueprint for Partnership and Growth*
Nayantara Sahgal (ed.)	*Before Freedom: Nehru's Letters to His Sister*
Rohan Gunaratna	*Inside Al Qaeda*
Eric S. Margolis	*War at the Top of the World*
Maj. Gen. Ian Cardozo	*Param Vir: Our Heroes in Battle*
Mushirul Hasan	*India Partitioned. 2 Vols*
Mushirul Hasan	*John Company to the Republic*
Mushirul Hasan	*Knowledge Power and Politics*
Ruskin Bond	*The Green Book*
Saad Bin Jung	*Wild Tales from the Wild*
Satish Jacob	*From Hotel Palestine Baghdad*

FORTHCOMING TITLES:

Dr Verghese Kurien with Gouri Salvi	*I Too Had a Dream*
Sharmistha Mohanty	*New Life*

cross-border talks

divided by
DEMOCRACY

meghnad desai
aitzaz ahsan

series editor
david page

Lotus Collection

© *Why is India a Democracy?*: Meghnad Desai, 2005
 Why Pakistan is not a Democracy: Aitzaz Ahsan, 2005
All rights reserved. No part of this publication may be reproduced or transmitted, in any form or by any means, without the prior permission of the publisher.

This edition first published in 2005
The Lotus Collection
An imprint of
Roli Books Pvt. Ltd.
M-75, G.K. II Market
New Delhi 110 048
Phones: ++91 (011) 2921 2271, 2921 2782
2921 0886, Fax: ++91 (011) 2921 7185
E-mail: roli@vsnl.com; Website: rolibooks.com
Also at
Bangalore, Varanasi, Jaipur and the Netherlands

Cover design: Arati Subramanyam
Layout design: Kumar Raman

ISBN: 81-7436-425-0
Rs 295/-

Typeset in Minion by Roli Books Pvt. Ltd. and printed at Syndicate Binders, Noida - 201305

contents

introduction 1
david page

why is india a democracy? 13
meghnad desai

why pakistan is not a democracy 75
aitzaz ahsan

introduction

david page

When the first volume in the *Cross-border Talks* series was published, it was making an argument for improved understanding between India and Pakistan, which was noticeable by its absence at that time. So much so that the launch of that volume – *Diplomatic Divide* by Dr Humayun Khan and G. Parthasarathy – in April 2004 in Delhi and Islamabad became something of a diplomatic event in its own right.

At that time, relations were only just beginning to improve after a sustained period of armed tension and hostility, which began with the Kargil conflict of 1999 and prompted fears of another full-scale war. Fortunately, the Kargil confrontation remained localized to the disputed territory of Kashmir but coming, as it did, only a year after India and Pakistan exploded nuclear devices, it was not surprising that it provoked widespread international concern. At that time, there was a palpable fear that their long-standing rivalry might escalate into nuclear war and bring disaster to the region as a whole.

Today, relations are much improved. After a meeting of the leaders of the two countries at the SAARC summit in January

2004, a gradual thaw has taken place. This has put diplomatic relations back onto a more normal footing and set in train a number of bilateral negotiations aimed at improving travel, communication, tourism and trade. Buses are now running not only from Delhi to Lahore but even from Srinagar to Muzzaffarabad. Indeed, Kashmiri politicians from the Valley travelled this route for the first time in decades when making a visit to Pakistan in mid-2005. These new links between the Kashmiri communities on different sides of the line of control are perhaps the most dramatic sign of a more positive approach to détente. Differences over the status of the former princely state remain unresolved but both countries have seen the value of making progress on other fronts as a means of building confidence for the future.

This progress has been particularly important in terms of people to people contact. In recent years, there have been a number of important initiatives to promote greater understanding, including what is called 'Track Three diplomacy' and exchange visits of various kinds. Many worthwhile contacts have been developed but progress has always been subject to the ups and downs of diplomatic relations. During times of tension, it has not been easy to obtain visas even to visit relatives, let alone for business or tourism. In the late 1970s and early 1980s, the two governments actually encouraged visits as an act of policy but only for a relatively short period. It is very good news, therefore, that there are now plans to reopen the consulates general in Karachi and Mumbai, which were shut down in 1993. This should greatly facilitate travel for those living in southern Pakistan and western India. Both governments have also been much less restrictive recently in granting visas for professional and personal travel, which has greatly increased the scope of cross-border contacts.

Advances in communication technologies have also played a part in bringing people together. The Internet has circumvented official restrictions and brought the possibility of more or less instant contact, though its impact remains confined to the computer-using classes. Among the general public, satellite television has done a great deal to break down barriers and to counter the stereotypes propagated for many years by the state-controlled media. But until recently the flow of images has been largely one-way – from India outwards – and increasingly open to government control, as the Kargil war showed, because of the growing consolidation and regulation of cable networks.

The *Cross-border Talks* series seeks to improve understanding of the issues which divide the two countries. It is aimed at members of the reading public on both sides of the border and its objective is to provide them with informed analysis of the issues which daily occupy the headlines. Among the issues scheduled for future debate are the nuclearization of South Asia, the faultlines of nationalism, the growth of fundamentalism, Kashmir, cricket, Jinnah's legacy, the cost of conflict, South Asian culture and economic relations.

There have been many books on Indo-Pakistan relations by nationals of the two countries but *Cross-border Talks* is probably the first series in which eminent Indians and Pakistanis systematically discuss the issues which divide them within the covers of one book. The series is also distinctive because each volume is published simultaneously in India and Pakistan in order to generate discussion in both countries at the same time.

The general format for the *Talks* is that the authors agree first on an agenda for discussion. They then write detailed treatments of the subject, which they exchange once completed. At this stage, they have an opportunity to revise their texts or to write brief rejoinders. In some cases, authors decide they do not wish to change their original statements. In others, they may take the opportunity to do so. We hope, however, that the debate between them will continue at the launches of the books and that this will engender a wider interest in the subject.

The first volume in the series, appropriately enough, was an analysis of bilateral relations by two senior retired diplomats who had worked with some of the key players and witnessed some of the moments of high tension and conflict in relations between Islamabad and Delhi. The second takes up an equally important issue – the progress of democracy in the two countries and the factors which have either facilitated or impeded its growth.

India is often characterized as the 'largest democracy' in the world, with an electorate of some 600 million voters who have a track record in recent years for changing governments with great regularity. India is also notable for the remarkable stability of its democratic institutions. There have been fourteen general elections in India since Independence in 1947 and only one brief period of Emergency rule, when the elected government was suspended nationally. Pakistan, on the other hand, has enjoyed far less continuity as a democratic country and has spent approximately half the time since Independence under different forms of military rule. There have been periods of democratic vitality – most notably in the 1970s and 1990s – but these have been relatively short-lived and have given way to military rule. Beginning with General Ayub's assumption of power in 1958, the Pakistan Army has played a very high-profile role in national politics and has provided the country with a number of its presidents, including General Zia-ul-Haq and General Pervez Musharraf.

Why India has succeeded in establishing democracy and why Pakistan has found it more difficult is the subject of this volume, which is authored by Meghnad Desai and Aitzaz Ahsan. Both men are eminently well placed to provide answers. Desai is an academic economist with a global reputation. Born and educated in India, he has spent the last forty years at the London School of Economics, where he founded and directed the Centre for the Study of Global Governance. He is also an active politician in Britain's Labour Party and a member of the House of Lords. Aitzaz Ahsan is one of Pakistan's most popular and forthright politicians, who has experienced the vicissitudes of democracy at first hand. Educated at Downing College, Cambridge, and the Inns of Court in London, he is a lawyer by training, with a successful commercial and criminal practice, and a long-standing commitment to human rights. He is also a leading member of the Pakistan People's Party. He served as home minister in the first cabinet of Benazir Bhutto and has held a number of other cabinet posts.

Meghnad Desai's concise account of the development of Indian democracy begins in the nineteenth century with the efforts of Indian politicians to persuade a reluctant Raj to introduce Westminster-style institutions in India. As someone with a deep knowledge of British political life himself, he sees the seeds of contemporary Indian democracy in the proliferation of Indian political associations on the British model and the dedication to the rule of law of Indian politicians educated in the Inns of Court in England. Though the Congress subsequently boycotted the official legislatures and embarked on a path of agitation against the British, he argues that these legislatures played a very important parallel role as a training ground for parliamentary practice.

In his account of the post-Partition period, Desai agrees with many other commentators in putting Nehru's contribution to Indian democracy on a high pedestal. India's gain from Nehru's patient nurturing of democratic practice during his long incumbency as the country's first prime minister contrasts with Pakistan's cruel loss in the early death of Muhammad Ali Jinnah, the founding father of the state and himself a lawyer in the same mould as many early Congress pioneers.

However, the main thrust of Desai's argument for the persistence of Indian democracy lies less in the liberal credentials of western-educated lawyers and politicians than in the revolutionary impact of the decision made after Independence to introduce universal adult suffrage. The role of the liberal lawyers may have been important in establishing democratic practice but their influence inevitably became diluted once the poor, the backward and the socially shunned were added to the electoral register. What requires explanation, he says, is how these disadvantaged groups came to see democracy as a means of their own empowerment and how the Indian political system settled down to what he calls 'a cosy accommodation with the local society, with its caste hierarchies, religious groupings and regional diversities'.

Desai attempts an answer to this question by a careful analysis of political developments from the early days of Congress dominance to the present-day world of multi-party national coalitions. In the first two decades after Independence, on the back of its strong nationalist credentials, the Congress successfully ruled both at the Centre and in the states and enjoyed an effective monopoly of power. But with the growing maturity of electoral politics, the Congress fragmented and other parties representing different linguistic, ethnic and caste interests emerged. From the late 1960s onwards, Congress's power was progressively diluted at the state level and a decade later, after India's experience of Indira Gandhi's Emergency, it was defeated nationally as well.

Desai charts the decline of single-party national governments and the emergence of multi-party coalitions at the Centre, most recently led by either the BJP or the Congress, which as national parties are themselves now fighting to maintain a dwindling share of the vote. He also charts the parallel growth of new parties appealing to disadvantaged castes first in the south and later in the north. As a political analyst, he is impressed by the way in which the decline of single-party dominance paved the way for politicians like Laloo Prasad Yadav to emerge as chief minister of Bihar or for a Dalit party to come to power in Uttar Pradesh, India's most populous state.

Desai also makes the argument that India's social divisions – which the proliferation of such caste parties now more accurately reflects – are themselves a guarantee against the domination of national politics by any particular religious, ethnic, regional or caste group. He acknowledges the fears of sectarianism generated in India after the destruction of the Babri Masjid in 1992 and the more recent outrage caused by the role of the Gujarat state government in the bloody killings in that state in March 2002. But writing after the surprising election result of 2004, which brought the defeat of the BJP-led coalition and the return to power of a Congress-led coalition, he argues that such fears were never wholly justified. In his view, India's political arithmetic would never support the emergence of a purely Hindutva government and the BJP, whatever its own convictions, would always be obliged to moderate its position to take account of these realities if it wished to form a government.

As an economist, however, Meghnad Desai is clear that India has paid a price for the political benefits of a fragmented polity. Caste politicians have diverted state finances and allocated public sector jobs to their own communities. But the results have often been economically disastrous for the state. Liberalization may have resulted in a transformation of the so-called Hindu rate of growth but in his view India would make much more progress economically and have a far greater surplus to distribute to the mass of the people if there was more political consensus at the national level. His scenarios for the future involve some stark choices and a surprising suggestion for a new form of coalition politics.

Aitzaz Ahsan brings to his analysis of Pakistani politics some of the same qualities and aspirations which inspired the liberal politicians of nineteenth century India. Called to the Bar at London's Gray's Inn, he clearly identifies with the professional skill and values of Jinnah, who was called to the Bar at Lincoln's Inn some seventy years earlier. Like many Pakistanis of a liberal persuasion, he draws strength from Jinnah's landmark statement to the Constituent Assembly on the eve of Independence in which he clearly set out his view that religion has 'nothing to do with the business of the state'. Like Jinnah himself, he clearly believes the law should be a guarantor of equality for all Pakistanis, whatever their caste or creed or sect.

Ahsan's analysis of the barriers to the establishment of a full fledged democracy in Pakistan reflects his own deep reading and thinking – much of it done during spells in Pakistan's jails – about what makes Pakistan's experience so different from that of India. This resulted some ten years ago in the publication of his well-known work, *The Indus Saga and the Making of Pakistan,* in which he elaborates his view that there always have been differences between the culture of the Indus region (which is now incorporated into Pakistan) and the region now known as India.

Much of that book deals with the early history of the Indus region – dating back to the Indus civilization of Mohenjo Daro, which, by contrast with those Pakistanis of an Islamist or fundamentalist persuasion, Ahsan happily recognizes as an ancient antecedent of the present-day state. In fact, one of the reasons the book has attracted so much interest is because it flatly rejects the idea that Pakistan's emergence was merely the result of a short-lived political movement and a series of inconclusive negotiations on the eve of Independence. In his view, 'distinctness of culture and economic disparities' were quite as important as religion in driving the countries apart. His reassuring message is that far from being a fragile state with a very short history, Pakistan as a region has a long and distinctive history of its own.

When it comes to assigning responsibility for the shortcomings of Pakistani democracy, however, Aitzaz Ahsan points the finger not at the ancient civilizations of the Indus valley but at the more recent impact of British imperial rule in the Punjab and neighbouring territories. The role of the Punjab as a military recruiting ground for the Raj is well known. From the time of the Great Uprising of 1857, the colonial authorities relied on what Ahsan calls 'the Indus soldier' to defend and police the empire. Compared with other provinces of India, the Punjab contributed a vastly disproportionate number of soldiers to the imperial armies, serving on the battlefields of Flanders in the First World War and in the North African campaigns of the Second. What is less well known, however, is that many thousand hectares of land brought into cultivation in the Punjab as a result of major irrigation works built by the Raj were distributed as rewards to military personnel and to those like horse and mule breeders who provided vital support services. Even the dominant political party in the Punjab between the two world wars – the Unionist Party – which brought together agriculturalists of all the main religious communities – was kept united to a very large extent by a shared reliance on the military patronage of the Indian Army.

Ahsan is in no doubt that this distortion of the purposes and responsibilities of the state in colonial times established a 'demarcation between democracy and praetorianism' which has proved a negative inheritance for Pakistan. If the Pakistan Army remains today a dominant force in the politics of the country, it is in large measure because Pakistan inherited a disproportionately large army and machinery of state accustomed to serving military purposes. But he carries this analysis one stage further, arguing, on the basis of his own wide experience, that the pervasiveness of military influence and the dependence of so many elements of Pakistani life on state patronage have drastically reduced the space for civil society to develop and impeded the growth of democratic institutions.

For any democracy to flourish and inspire confidence in its citizens, there have to be regular elections, political consensus on how institutions work and a credible judiciary to uphold the constitution or arbitrate in the event of disputes. Though Pakistan has experienced democracy over many years, one significant reflection of its lack of democratic maturity is that in nearly sixty years there never has been a smooth change of government following a general election. Even in the period from 1988 to 1999, when there were four general elections and four different governments, each government came to an abrupt end, dismissed either by presidential intervention or by military coup. There could not be a bigger contrast with Indian experience, where there is now a well-established tradition of general elections resulting in changes of government.

Both Meghnad Desai and Aitzaz Ahsan highlight the role of the judiciary in safeguarding democracy, though here again the experience of the two countries is very different. Desai acknowledges that certain politicians in India have sought to manipulate the judiciary by transfers of judges and other means. However, he argues that despite some trends towards corruption in the lower courts, the Indian Supreme Court remains a powerful and effective watchdog in safeguarding the Constitution and protecting the rights of the citizens.

Aitzaz Ahsan, an eminent Supreme Court lawyer himself, devotes considerable space to the role of the judiciary in Pakistan's own democratic progress. By and large, it is a critical review, which shows that despite the commitment of many fine judges and barristers in Pakistan to the principles of judicial independence, the Supreme Court has more often than not provided legitimacy for the coup-makers and, in however qualified a way, sided with those already in power.

Though the two authors approach their subjects with different perspectives and expertise, they provide two very stimulating analyses of the strengths and weaknesses of Indian and Pakistani democracies. India certainly has more to celebrate in terms of political maturity and social transformation, though Desai acknowledges that what he calls 'the roulette wheel' of Indian politics is not working very well in delivering economic benefits to the citizens at large. Ahsan can point to far less progress in terms of social and political emancipation. But the

INTRODUCTION 11

two men agree on the vital importance of universal adult suffrage as the means of empowerment and a vehicle for social change. Pakistanis have had less opportunity than Indians to exercise their vote but they value it just as highly, and however interrupted their experience of democracy, this remains a reality their political masters cannot ignore.

London
June 2005

David Page
Series Editor

why is india a democracy?

meghnad desai

'... *but India is the only democratic land in the world.*'
— Rudyard Kipling, *Kim*

The elections held in May 2004 brought India and its democracy to global attention. The reasons were many, but two main ones can be cited. Firstly, India's successful efforts at economic reform and coping with globalization were making it a country of interest to overseas investors. India was economic news for these people. But the more important reason was the unexpected outcome. Most people – experts, media commentators, academics, politicians – had predicted the re-election of the National Democratic Alliance (NDA), a coalition of a dozen parties led by the BJP. With the economy booming, the coalition's slogan 'India Shining' sounded persuasive. Instead, Congress and its coalition of eighteen parties won by a narrow margin. Indian democracy became a matter of interest to a much wider audience than had been the case till now.

Yet India has been a democracy since Independence. There have been general elections at the national level since 1952. The latest one was the fourteenth general election with upward of 600 million voters in twenty-eight states and three union territories. The outcome was made up of a complex tapestry of results at the state level with many small regional and caste parties determining the balance. Incumbent governments lost in many states – Congress governments as much as BJP governments. Deciphering the reasons why one party won and the other did not required that one knew the caste and religious mix of the local parties and their allegiance to one or the other major parties – BJP or Congress. There followed a debate on whether the verdict meant a rejection of the economic reforms the outgoing government had been pursuing or of the communalist, i.e. anti-Muslim stance, that some of its supporters, especially in the state of Gujarat, had adopted during the riots in March 2002.

Perhaps most impressive of all was the fact that an election involving such a large number of voters, many of them illiterate and some living in remote areas, had been conducted peacefully and fairly, using electronic voting machines and voter identity cards. The polling itself was spread out over weeks and the count was not made till all the rounds of voting had been completed. Everything worked in a clockwork fashion in a country where the locals are the first to deride their own ability to organize even a small event efficiently. Yet India conducted an election with more modern equipment and fewer doubts about the legitimacy of the process than, for example, the USA in 2000 or even 2004.

What explains this achievement? Why has India, among the many post-colonial societies, succeeded in maintaining a democratic polity when others all around have been tempted by and succumbed to the authoritarian alternative? This is especially true of its twin Pakistan with whom India was joined until Independence as a British colony. It is true that Sri Lanka has maintained a democratic culture in the midst of civil war and Bangladesh reverted to democracy after a lurch into dictatorship. But the other ex-British colony, Burma (Myanmar), has gone the same way. In Africa, many ex-British colonies, including Nigeria, Ghana, Uganda and Sierra Leone, have had a chequered experience with democracy. Similar cases could be cited in Francophone Africa or Latin America. India, on the other hand, as a fifty-plus-year-old democracy, is among the older ones in the world – Spain, Portugal, Greece and even Germany are younger than India as democracies, to say nothing of the countries of Eastern Europe or the constituents of the former Soviet Union.

Why should a country, a quarter of whose population is poor, half of whose children are malnourished, with a substantial minority of its men and even more of its women illiterate, which is riven by ethnic, religious and caste divisions, where feudal and semi-feudal relations persist in some rural parts, whose social structure is marked by a hierarchical ordering recognized as an epitome of inegalitarianism, achieve a democratic polity?

In what follows I shall try and present an explanation. Given the need for brevity, I shall keep references to academic works and citations of any statistics to a minimum. This is as far as possible my own explanation, though I lay no claim to originality. I do not spend any words on things like a general definition of democracy or the types of democracy. During the course of the essay, I shall make clear what type of democracy India is and whether it is the best form of democracy India can have.

The first section after this introduction lays out the historical forces during the pre-Independence period, which sowed the seeds of what later became the democratic polity in India. This is mainly about the Independence struggle and the role the Congress played in it. The next section examines the choices before independent India and the decision to adopt a democratic framework with universal adult franchise and a federal structure of government. The third describes the course of Indian democracy over the first thirty years after the adoption of the Constitution. The purpose of stopping in 1977 is to mark an end to the only attempt to abridge India's democracy, that was tried by Indira Gandhi. Its failure sealed the authoritarian impulse in Indian politics for the foreseeable future. The fourth section pauses in the narrative and asks whether there were systemic reasons why India survived as a democracy. Here we examine some of the issues discussed previously in the light of the experience of the first thirty years. We observe that democracy as it took shape in India was more suited to local conditions than could have been anticipated. The fifth section looks at the course of democracy over the next twenty-seven years and shows how India's democracy is embedded in the contradictions of its social structure and why this strengthens rather than weakens it. The sixth will make a critique of Indian democracy, keeping in mind what it has achieved and how much it has disappointed its champions. The last section will look briefly at the future of Indian democracy. I wish to thank Katharine Adeney and Kishwar Desai for carefully reading earlier drafts and suggesting improvements and David Page for patient and careful editing.

the long apprenticeship: 1858-1947

Power was transferred from the East India Company to Her Majesty's Government by an Act of Parliament in 1858. This was accompanied by a Proclamation by Queen Victoria, which promised to treat all her subjects in a neutral and impartial fashion respecting their religions and assuring them that their religious practices will be free of molestation. The Proclamation became something of a 'Magna Carta of our rights and privileges' in the eyes of the new educated middle class of Victorian India. The members of this class had been trained in the three universities established at the three port cities of Calcutta, Bombay and Madras. It was this class, tiny in proportion to the total population of around 180 million but still numerically large, which was to play a crucial role in the development of public political life in India.

The members of this class had absorbed English history, mostly in Macaulay's florid Whig version, and devoured parliamentary speeches as they were reported in the fledgling English language press. They were loyal to the Crown and wanted nothing more than being able to speak like their idols, Burke and Charles James Fox, and the Elder and the Younger Pitt. They studied contemporary British politics in great detail. The majority of this contingent was favourable to the policies of the Liberal Party rather than its rival, the Conservative Party. Even before the century was over, however, Indians had sat in the House of Commons, one each for the Liberals and for the Conservatives.

During the fifty odd years following the 1858 transfer of power, there was a veritable orgy of forming organizations for purposes of reform of religion and society in India, in which these middle class professionals took a leading part. There was the Brahmo Samaj in Calcutta and the Prarthana Samaj in Bombay; there were the Sarvajanik Sabha and Hindu Mahamandal in smaller towns. The one feature they had in common was that they were organized along the lines of associations in Britain as the Indian middle classes understood them. There were written constitutions, elections of officers, formal meetings with speeches and resolutions. These organizations would present petitions and pass resolutions of loyal support on the occasion of royal birthdays. They proved to be a training ground of sorts where Indians were acquainted with novel forms of organization and with the grammar in which political life was to be conducted.

The spread of railways during these fifty years gave the new elite a way of getting together. While the idea of India as a cultural entity had always been there, its territorial extent had never been determined. Once the Afghan adventure had come to an end and the Durand line was drawn, India as a territorial unit was given a definite shape. Now rail travel brought home to its users the vastness of India as well as its interconnectedness. Calcutta, Bombay and Madras were not just the capitals of Presidencies but cities of a new emerging India. It was an India over which a parliamentary democracy ruled in an unparliamentary fashion. The elite thus took to articulating their demands in the style of their rulers as they could best emulate them and began demanding, ever so politely at first, an end to 'Un-British' rule. They were scrupulous in following all the trappings of democratic discourse, which they had learned from their English books. They were keen to show that they were representatives of a larger collectivity and also that their conduct showed that they deserved to be trusted with parliamentary governance.

Thus, even before the founding of the Congress party in 1885, there was an attempt to imbibe democratic practices as the elite perceived them to operate in the imperial homeland. They had no clear agenda of what shape their parliament would take or what powers it would have. But they very much wanted to prove that they had earned their right to be treated at par with Her Imperial Majesty's subjects as she had promised. They studied the governance of other colonies, Canada for one, and observed the movements for Home Rule in Ireland. They aspired to be like those other parts of the Empire. They formed the Congress to pursue their claim.

In her apprenticeship for democracy, India was fortunate to have the Congress as a broad umbrella organization to begin with. For the first twenty years of its existence, it came into life only at its annual meetings in December for three or four days, heard speeches, passed resolutions and then subsided as the delegates went back to their comfortable homes. Yet the Congress met in different cities of India and recruited the local elites of these towns and cities into the organization as local committee members and delegates. It became this way an all-

India body, the label itself suggesting the novelty of any organization that spanned the entire country.

The Congress changed from a docile loyalist organization to a more noisy, dissenting one during the agitation of 1905 against the partition of Bengal. Its leadership, still middle class, displayed in their attire a greater diversity of local dresses and in their speeches some strong religious imagery taken from Hinduism and Islam. But even as it did this, its democratic procedures and practices did not change. Soon after the radicalization of the Congress, in 1909 there came an opportunity in the form of the Morley-Minto reforms to win representation in the various councils at provincial level, in which the Indians could practise being parliamentarians, albeit with very limited constituencies and practically no powers compared to their beloved House of Commons. Even before this, some Indians had been invited to serve on the Imperial Legislative Council as non-official members. They had position but no power. But at least the few who had that status had early training in being parliamentarians.

Thus, there were two fora for practising democracy in the political sphere. There was the Congress and other organizations such as the Muslim League where speeches were made and resolutions passed. And there were the legislative councils at provincial and imperial levels where the co-opted or elected members could play at being parliamentarians. In the subsequent historiography of the Independence movement as dictated by the Congress Party, the official legislatures have been downplayed and all virtue has been attributed to the Congress and its agitational activities under the leadership of Gandhi. But as a training ground for parliamentary practices and for the development of a democratic culture, the two paths – constitutional and agitational – were equally important.

What the Congress under Gandhi's leadership did was to extend this experience of democratic procedures and practices to a much wider mass of people, way beyond the educated middle class elite. Elections within the Congress at provincial or district level now became meaningful exercises. Delegates to the Congress annual conferences were elected from their grass-roots committees. They arrived at the annual sessions and learned the art of moving resolutions and voting on them, and of electing their officers (though strongly guided by their leader, the Mahatma). Meanwhile the constitutional forum expanded in scope even as the Congress was divided on the merits of joining it. The Montagu-Chelmsford Reforms of 1919 introduced an element of popular government at provincial level, though effective power was still retained by the British appointees. Within a decade, constitutional discussions began again in Round Table Conferences held in London and these discussions soon developed into the Government of India Act of 1935. This act extended the franchise and the powers of elected members at the provincial level. In 1937, elections were held in eleven provinces in which the Congress along with the Muslim League, the Hindu Mahasabha and other parties participated (I take up some of these developments in greater detail below).

There were also by then municipalities in many towns and cities where the elective principle was followed, and many local people practised the arts of democracy. Organizations for social reform also multiplied and spread the procedures of democratic behaviour further into the population. Many of the social reform organizations were concerned with the reform of Hindu society. The elite castes were as much concerned with cleansing the image of Hinduism as were the lower castes and the untouchables in radically challenging its tenets. The associations in the North were mainly upper caste ones with an agenda of purifying but reasserting the orthodox religion. But as you moved south, there was a preponderance of lower caste and untouchable movements, which were by and large anti- Brahminical and wanted an overhaul of orthodox practices.

Either way, the path was strewn with resolutions and petitions and memoranda. Among the Muslim population, there was a delay before the community took to Western education and a lack of urgency about religious or social reform. This was because the Muslim community was part of a much larger community of Muslims which stretched beyond India and also because Islam had not been subjected to the same harsh criticism as Hinduism by the English Utilitarians, following the lead given by the economist James Mill in his *History of British India*.

Thus by the time Independence arrived in 1947, Indians had a lot of experience of democratic procedures and practices. They were used to elections and voting, to moving, debating and passing resolutions and, what is more, of abiding by them. The Mahatma was often the exception to the rule and resorted to a fast when he did not get his way or strong-armed a candidate out if he did not approve of his election, as he did with Subhash Bose in 1938. But his position was unique, and, apart from him, everyone else behaved in a rule-abiding way. This was particularly true of Jawaharlal Nehru, whose attitude towards proper procedures was to be a crucial ingredient of India's democratic culture after Independence. But along with him were others, many of them barristers, who were scrupulous about wording of resolutions and their implementation.

Democracy is not merely formal procedures of parliamentary behaviour and the practice of elections. But it has to be that at least before it can be anything else. Dictators have often preferred models of 'basic' democracy with indirect elections or party-free arrangements. The so-called People's Democracies are one-party affairs. But they are shams, whatever their other virtues may be. A formal commitment to free elections and open debate, with voting of resolutions, which then form the action plan of the organization, is a totally necessary ingredient of a democratic culture. It has to be possible to replace a government with an alternative. The rulers have to be subject to the same laws as the opposition – as liable to being dismissed as capable of being re-elected. It is when we see dictators deny even this formal minimum that we see democracy's potential subversive power.

With the Congress being an umbrella organization rather than a monolithic party through much of its first sixty years, there was never any danger that it would become a dictatorial party, even discounting the Mahatma's passion for control. Its existence and evolution into a mass party prepared Indians for a democratic future. Yet as Independence approached, there were siren voices warning against any sudden lurch towards democracy. The fact that India did in fact adopt a democratic republican constitution was not a foregone conclusion. It was the deliberations of the Constituent Assembly which determined the outcome. It is to that which I now turn.

crucial choices/wise leadership

Once the war ended, it was obvious that sooner rather than later, India would be independent. In the British elections of 1945, the Labour Party had surprised everyone by coming to power with a substantial majority. Winston Churchill, long an opponent of Indian independence, was defeated and Clement Attlee became prime minister. There had been discussions about a new constitutional arrangement for India through Second World War and these resumed after the war. Two things became clear. One was that upon independence, there would be two units not one. Partition was and remains a controversial issue but it is not the matter under discussion here. The second development was that independent India would have to frame its own constitution. It had to fashion its own future.

An election took place in 1946 based on a limited franchise for the legislature that would double as a Constituent Assembly. In this election, the division between the Muslim League and the Congress became clear. Except for the North West Frontier Province, the Congress did not win any of the provinces where there was a Muslim majority population. Thus the new legislature, which was to write India's constitution, was predominantly Congress-based, though in an ecumenical gesture, various non-Congress leaders such as Dr Ambedkar were given seats. As far as possible, the Assembly was to represent the whole country. The real issue then was: what sort of constitution did India want to have for itself?

To some extent, discussions on the Indian constitution had been taking place throughout the 20th century. The British government had introduced a series of constitutional reforms to give a limited amount of governance to Indians. The Morley-Minto reforms of 1909 were followed by the Montagu-Chelmsford reforms of 1919. Then a commission was appointed under the chairmanship of John Simon to report on the progress of the 1919 reforms. The Simon commission was boycotted everywhere it went in India but one of its members, Clement Attlee, was able to draw his own conclusions from his visit. The Simon Commission's report was set aside by the British government, which committed itself in a statement by the Viceroy Lord Irwin to work towards Dominion Status for India. Although the Congress rejected this as inadequate, there followed three Round Table Conferences. It was at these conferences that various sections of India – religions, provinces, women, untouchables, native princes – were represented for the first time in a consultative capacity. It was at the first conference that a proposal was put forward by one of the princes that India should be constituted as a confederation. This idea took root and after five more years of legislative deliberation by both houses of the British parliament the Government of India Bill, 1935 became an act. It proposed that India would be a federation with the British provinces as well as the princely states being members, with direct elections to the Lower House and indirect representation in the Council of States, the Upper

House. There was to be a division of subjects between the Centre and the states but the states were to have a lot of autonomy within the overall control of military, currency and foreign affairs by the Centre. There were Schedules listing backward castes and tribes which were to merit special treatment.

The Government of India Act of 1935 set down the mainframe of independent India's Constitution. But there were some changes. Firstly, rather than the native states being independent members of the federation, they were absorbed into provinces of independent India. This was a revolutionary step. The native states were not fully sovereign but were under the paramountcy of the British crown as represented by the viceroy. Upon Independence, the paramountcy could have lapsed, leaving the native states, some of which were large enough to be countries in their own right – Hyderabad, Mysore, Jammu and Kashmir – as sovereign. However, Mountbatten, as the last viceroy, made it clear just months before Indian independence that the native states had to choose between joining India or Pakistan but with very limited real choice. Proximity to one or the other new country would be the deciding factor. Most joined without fuss one or the other. Only Jammu and Kashmir proved to be an anomaly since it was on the border of both the newly separated nations and could have joined either. But Hari Singh, a Hindu prince with a majority Muslim population (abetted by Sheikh Abdullah who wanted to remove him and establish a people's government) played for time. He regretted it when some irregulars from over the Pakistan border marched on Srinagar, his capital. He signed up with India but this precipitated a war between the two new nations and an appeal to the recently established UN, followed by a rather messy result: Kashmir was divided by a 'line of control' but with no solution as to its governance. The 'Kashmir issue' is still a bone of contention between the two countries, with India sure of its rights as the legitimate authority with whom the prince signed an agreement and Pakistan claiming that the issue of Kashmir is unresolved until there is a plebiscite of its people. Kashmir has been the cause of at least three wars between the two nations.

After Independence, Sardar Patel as the home minister cajoled the native princes and in some cases (the Nizam of Hyderabad, for instance) strong-armed them into merging with the nearby parts of what was previously British India and now was under the rule of the new government in Delhi. Kashmir was given a special autonomous status in the Constitution. Independent India thus began as a single sovereign power. The new government in Delhi therefore became the first in India's long history to rule over all of India, albeit minus the parts that went to Pakistan.[1]

Secondly, the division of powers between the Centre and the states was not to be as envisaged in the Act – a weak Centre and strong states. Congress was committed to a strong central authority. Indeed the very idea of a federation rather than a unitary arrangement was accepted reluctantly. Independent India, recently partitioned, was wary of balkanization and wanted to guard against it.

Thus India was to be a united entity with a single sovereignty rather than burdened with 600 native states. But then what? From the very beginning of the independence movement, Indian leaders were besotted with the Westminster model and its bicameral structure was adopted but with the obvious change that the Upper House would not be a hereditary chamber but an indirectly elected one. The lower house would be directly elected. The question was of the franchise – how wide and with what reservations and separations?

It was here that the Constituent Assembly made its most revolutionary decision. It chose universal adult franchise. In doing so, it was setting aside all sorts of objections based on tradition or even reason that could have been advanced. It should be remembered that women had been granted a vote on the same basis as men only during the inter-war period in the USA and UK and only in 1945 in France. But the Congress had always been open to women as members and some had become leaders – Sarojini Naidu, Amrit Kaur, Aruna Asaf Ali among others. Thus the Congress was wedded to a sort of formal equality in political participation. It was also a bold decision not to insist on a literacy criterion in a country with an illiterate majority in its population. There were to be no separate electorates by religion, a topic which had been controversial throughout the previous thirty years. There were to be reserved seats for the Scheduled Castes.

The adoption of universal adult franchise was a revolutionary step just because nothing in Indian history justified it. Ancient India had some examples of republics but the entire structure of Hindu society based on jatis (sub castes) and exclusion of untouchables dictated a hierarchical arrangement. An orthodox Hindu party would have surely excluded the untouchables and perhaps women as well. Furthermore, though it may seem obvious today, the choice of a republic was also novel. The previous great uprising against the British in 1857 was wedded to restoration of either a Mughal or a Maratha kingship. Within ninety years, India had travelled a long way to modernity.

The adoption of a modern democratic republican framework was fraught with dangers. It was not clear that a Westminster arrangement was suitable for India. The Communist Party of course wanted India to follow the Soviet constitution of 1935. There were some arguments for a US style presidential system. The Constituent Assembly was packed with lawyers and constitutional experts. Dr Ambedkar emerged as one of the principal architects of the Constitution. He had a doctorate in economics from the London School of Economics and one in law from Columbia University.

He had risen from untouchable status during the inter-war years, when no one would sit next to him or work with him, to become a leader of his community. The Assembly looked at many constitutions but chose as its model an unwritten one and proceeded to write down most of its features.

The Westminster-style Constitution, which India adopted, gave it a lower house of Parliament (Lok Sabha) elected directly by an electorate based on universal adult franchise. It then gave the majority party in the Lok Sabha extensive executive powers with few constraints. Thereby, India incorporated all the virtues and defects of the Westminster arrangement. The Lok Sabha became the centre of all political combat. The principle of majority party rule gave the winning party a lot of power and patronage. In the US constitution, there is a built-in antagonism between the executive and the legislature. The senate there especially exerts a powerful brake on the president's patronage in appointments and foreign relations. India, like the UK, adopted the unfettered executive as its model. The prime minister, popularly elected as head of the majority party, partakes of the Royal Prerogative and is unconstrained in his appointments and conduct of foreign affairs. This could lead to a dictatorship of a single party and of its leader in a new democracy without the conventions and historical memories which bind the House of Commons.

This tendency towards absolute executive domination was compounded by the decision to adopt a federal structure which was heavily biased towards a strong centre. Unlike in Australia and the United States, the individual states were creatures of the centre and not autonomous entities. Their boundaries could be altered and their popularly elected governments could be dismissed by the Centre. This was an echo of the Act of 1935.

India thus gave itself a democratic constitution with built-in autocratic tendencies. It could have made the majority leader a Bonapartist dictator if she had the necessary strength in the Lok Sabha. It is a possibility which was briefly realized in the course of the next fifty plus years. But the fact that India did not immediately lurch into a dictatorship owed much to the character of one man – Jawaharlal Nehru – and of the party he led – the Congress Party. Nehru was a democrat par excellence and the party he headed was an inclusive, broad-based one in which disparate interest groups and ethnic factions could happily coexist. It was also, as I argued earlier, a party used to a democratic way of decision-making, guided by a strong leader.

Nehru saw to it that the new democratic polity of India took deep roots in the first seventeen years after Independence while he was prime minister. It was a happy accident that he lasted that long. The element of continuity imparted by this fact cannot be exaggerated and is frequently underplayed. Pakistan by contrast did not have this good fortune, as Jinnah and Liaqat Ali Khan both died soon after Independence. Malaya was lucky, as a young independent country, to enjoy a similar long tenure of its first prime minister – Tunku Abdul Rahman – who ruled for thirteen years. But in other cases, the longevity of the original leader has not helped. Robert Mugabe of Zimbabwe and Jomo Kenyatta of Kenya come readily to mind. In Bangladesh, Sheikh Mujibur Rahman transformed from a democrat into a dictator quite rapidly.

What Nehru had was not just longevity but a deep personal commitment to democracy. This personal factor should not be underestimated, if only because it has become *au courant* to downgrade Nehru's contribution. Even during his tenure as prime minister, it was fashionable to say that Nehru was a like a large banyan tree under whose shade nothing grew. This was false since what grew was India's democracy. It was Nehru's scrupulous insistence on behaving on strictly procedural lines which set a model for subsequent behaviour.[2] He also wrote regularly to the chief ministers of states telling them about world events and decisions of national importance. This way he educated them in world politics and gave the federation a coherence it would not have acquired from the formal arrangements alone. His self-denial in not grabbing unlimited power and going back to the country on a regular five-year basis were important elements in building up a democratic culture in India. It does not sound like much, but if India did not go the way of Burma, Pakistan, Nigeria, Ghana or Zimbabwe, it is due to this happy accident. Nehru was the first among post-colonial leaders to lead a large country and he stayed a democrat. While none of his successors has measured up to his standards, the norm he set is still important. Having had nearly two decades of a democratic leadership at its start, India got addicted to democracy.

But there was also the 'Congress System', as one distinguished Indian political scientist, Rajni Kothari, has called it.[3] This was the inclusiveness of the Congress Party, which at the time of independence gave a place to all the major cleavages in Indian society. While its leadership was Hindu upper caste, there were also Muslims, untouchables, women and various regional and linguistic groups represented in its high offices. Congress had a nationwide organization with offices at provincial, district and even village levels. Opinion flowed up through the channels and patronage trickled down. At least until 1969, when Indira Gandhi split the party, the Congress system worked. This meant that many contentious issues could be solved within the party before they became cross-party issues.

But the Congress was also influential in as much as many of the parties formed after Independence had broken away from it. The Socialist Party was one such, which combined with another off-shoot, the Kisan Mazdoor Praja Party, and formed the Praja Socialist Party which performed as a loyal opposition. Other parties such as the Hindu Mahasabha – the Jan Sangh as it became later – predated Independence, as did the Communist Party. Thus at the first general elections, there was already a multi-party structure to contest Congress at the polls.

coping with pressures

Despite the good initial conditions described above, Indian democracy had still to cope with tremendous divisive pressures. Partition had already indicated that certain divisions are hard to contain within a Westminster style system where the winner takes all and the majority rules. Jinnah was worried that such a majority in an undivided India would be permanently Hindu to the detriment of Muslims. Whatever the salience of his doubts, the Hindu majority was also divided by caste, languages and regions. One hundred and fifty years of colonial rule had brought change and development at an uneven pace in different parts. Some communities and some regions had benefited while others had lagged behind. Now with democracy and electoral politics, these pressures could surface. Dr Ambedkar, as an architect of the Constitution and one acutely aware of the corrosive effects of inequality, warned that India was adopting a franchise system which presumed equality among voters while the reality was a pervasive economic and social inequality. There were tensions and contradictions inherent in such a situation. The Congress tried its best to contain these but in the process it succumbed to the pressures itself. But as it succumbed, the democratic nature of the Indian polity deepened rather than coming to any harm.

The first set of pressures came from linguistic groups. The colonial provincial boundaries had been drawn with no logic, and though Congress had initially organized its own provincial committees along those arbitrary lines, it was committed to a re-organization along linguistic lines. Soon after Independence, Nehru got cold feet and resisted any such reorganization, but the pressures from communities which had been held back became overwhelming. They argued that others, sometimes minorities, within 'their' territory had done better. They wanted to translate their numerical majority into an economic advantage via the ballot box. The latter half of the 1950s saw a tremendous movement, often of anti-Congress coalitions, to challenge Nehru. By 1960, the linguistic issue had been resolved and new states formed. But in the process, various regional sub-nationalisms articulated themselves. From now on, Congress had to look at the linguistic mix of its cabinets at Centre and state levels. Linguistic agitation strengthened oppositional forces and made a challenge to Congress more likely in the future. Disparate parties learnt to come together in temporary alliance against the Congress. One major socialist leader, Ram Manohar Lohia, articulated a doctrine that only by weakening the Congress would India thrive. Anti-Congressism as a political programme was born then and was to influence politics in subsequent decades.

The other major cleavage was between the North and the South. The four southern provinces – Andhra, Karnataka, Kerala and Tamil Nadu – form a Dravidian group with substantial differences from the North. The South had a strong anti-Brahmin tradition, especially in Tamil Nadu, where the Dravida Kazhagam, established by Ramaswami Naicker, gave the Dravidian identity a strong nationalistic flavour. The Congress was strongly challenged by the party that rose out of Naicker's movement, called the Dravida Munnetra Kazhagam (DMK). Through the 1950s, there was fear that the southern states might secede from the union.[4]

The conflict came to the surface on the question of making Hindi the sole national language after 1965, as had been envisaged in the Constitution. This would have put the southern regions at a disadvantage, especially in seeking and getting government jobs. A massive agitation broke out as the deadline approached and Lal Bahadur Shastri, Nehru's successor, was able to work out a compromise whereby the constitutional decision was never to be implemented. English and Hindi were to be the two national languages and the fourteen other languages listed in the Constitution would be official languages.

The 1960s witnessed multiple pressures on India. The defeat in the Indo-China border war in 1962 was eased by the better result in the Indo-Pakistan war of 1965. But there were two famines in the mid-1960s as well as the deaths of two prime ministers – Nehru and Shastri. The economy, which had grown well in the 1950s, began to run into trouble and the Third Five Year Plan (1961-66) yielded growth way below target. Food was in short supply and India became dependent on PL 480 food shipments from the United States. The rupee was devalued by the incoming prime minister, Mrs Indira Gandhi, and yet President Lyndon Johnson was able to stop the promised aid from the World Bank because of India's stance on Vietnam. Congress lost heavily in the 1967 elections, ceding several states to opposition parties.

Within the Congress itself, multiple centres of power had developed, thanks to the formation of linguistic states and the growth of regional elites. These regional leaders flexed their muscles when Mrs Gandhi became prime minister. They challenged the hegemony of the Delhi-based Centre as well as the Nehruvian doctrine of state-led industrialization. They favoured rural interests, especially agricultural ones, and preferred a watered down version of Nehruvian socialism.

Mrs Gandhi was able to reassert central power and her hegemony over the Congress by splitting the party and relying on the Communist parties for support in the parliament. She charted a radical path and nationalised the commercial banks. This won her the support of the Left. She called a mid-term election in early 1971 and won a majority. Soon after this, the breakaway movement in East Pakistan gave her a moment of triumph, as she was able to deploy Indian troops to aid the Bangladeshi *Mukti Bahini*. It looked as if the Congress, now split into Gandhi and anti-Gandhi factions, could revive its glory with the dominant faction alone. Trading on her name and her parentage, Indira Gandhi sought to consolidate dynastic power in democratic India.

A third source of tension was class-based cleavages. The Communist Party of India (CPI) had tried during an adventurist phase just after Independence to foment an agrarian revolt in the Telangana region of Andhra Pradesh. But this had failed and with it the dream of a Red Revolution had been abandoned by the International Communist movement. The party itself split due to larger pressures in the international movement during the 1960s. But a more radical faction, modelling itself on Chinese guerilla tactics, came to the fore in the tribal areas of West Bengal. The Naxalbari movement of the Communist Party Marxist-Leninist fought a sturdy battle in the countryside of West Bengal as well as in Calcutta. While it was contained, it has survived to these days in areas of rural India – Bihar and Andhra Pradesh especially – where tribal communities exist on the edge of poor agricultural settlements.

A fourth source of tension was based on an intersection of caste and class. Two decades plus of slow economic growth (1 to 1.3 per cent per capita per annum) had left a lot of communities behind in the economic race. State-based development had created jobs for the well-educated upper caste/upper class English speaking elites, leaving behind lower castes, untouchables (Dalits) and tribals. These were the majority of the country but the democratic electoral machinery had not been used by them hitherto since they had looked to the Congress to represent them. Despite Indira Gandhi's slogan 'Garibi Hatao' (Remove Poverty), there had been no dent in India's poverty levels as measured.

The quadrupling of oil prices and the subsequent inflation lit the torch of this protest movement. In Gujarat, it became a popular agitation against inflation and government corruption. Nava Nirman (New dispensation) was a loose coalition of community groups and political parties. It was led by the veteran socialist, Jaya Prakash Narayan. Soon a nationwide railwaymen's strike followed which had to be put down. Indira Gandhi was then challenged in a court of law about irregularities in her election campaign. To her surprise, she lost the case and was ordered to resign her position. She chose thereupon to declare a State of Emergency. It looked as if Indian democracy, so proudly hailed in the 1950s, was to end in 1975.

The opposition to the Emergency was led not by the Left, which supported Mrs Gandhi as a 'progressive bourgeois force', but by a motley collection of right wing and religious parties, regional formations, and social movements of tribals, Dalits and women. While repression was successful for a while, Mrs Gandhi behaved true to her father's heritage and called elections in 1977, which she lost. The end of the Emergency and the subsequent defeat in an election of the leader who had imposed it strengthened Indian democracy immensely.

India emerged at the end of the 1970s with its democratic structures in good shape. It had managed to weather crises on several fronts and accommodated various pressures arising from multiple cleavages. While the one-party dominance of the Congress lasted until 1967, the solutions sought for the problems faced by the nation were inclusive and consensual. It was only after Congress hegemony was challenged and the party had to be rebuilt by Mrs Gandhi that insecurity set in. Mrs Gandhi's solutions were confrontational or, as she and her Left friends tried to label them, radical. Having faced the demise of the Congress in many provincial governments, she fought hard to retain its hold on power at the Central level. It was in this effort that she over-reached herself. The Emergency failed to tackle India's problems. It showed that only inclusive solutions work in a polity addicted to democracy. Pakistan went through a similar crisis of a challenge to the hegemony of the old elite in 1970 when Mujibur Rahman won a majority in the elections in Pakistan. But there was no inclusive solution and the effort to maintain the hegemony of West Pakistan's elite broke the union.

In India, the hegemony of the Congress had been successfully challenged. Anti-Congressism had its biggest triumph to date in overthrowing a Congress government not just at state level but at the Centre itself. The Janata government, which came to power in 1977, was a coalition of many factions – the minority Congress (Nijalingappa), Jan Sangh, various remnants of the splintered Praja Socialist Party and the Swatantra Party. The minority Congress faction consisted of regional leaders who had been thrown out by Mrs Gandhi – Charan Singh, the north Indian Jat leader, Sanjiva Reddy of Andhra Pradesh and Nijalingappa of Karnataka. The Jan Sangh was a right wing Hindu party which had a small presence in Indian politics until the Emergency. But it was now helped by its role in the anti-Gandhi struggle and emerged as a popular party. It entrenched itself and expanded, renaming itself as the Bharatiya Janata Party. The Swatantra Party was a secular right-wing liberal party. India's multiple party structure, rather than simplifying into a two-party system, flowered further. It is this flowering of the multiple parties which was to determine the dynamics of Indian democracy in the coming decades. This was despite the fact that the Janata Government did not last long and in the 1979/1980 election, Mrs Gandhi and her Congress were returned to power for a decade of hegemony.

why did democracy survive in india?

By 1980, India had had seven general elections over twenty-eight years. It had seen five prime ministers and two changes of the party in power at the Centre. In the individual states, the Congress monopoly had slipped much earlier: in 1957, when the Communists came to power in Kerala, and more generally after the elections in 1967. In 1977, however, the Congress monopoly of power had been broken at the Centre, though not for long. India had come close to lapsing into a dictatorship, from which it was saved perhaps by the self-delusion of Indira Gandhi about her popularity, since there was an attempt to muzzle the press during the Emergency.

Was Democracy a stable and permanent feature of Indian polity or was it just a temporary arrangement? By 1980, Pakistan had swung back and forth between democracy and dictatorship many times. Bangladesh witnessed the first flush of popular rule only to see it reversed by Mujibur Rahman's dictatorship. But this is not only a Third World problem. Fifteen years after the inauguration of the Fourth Republic, France had witnessed its collapse, the return of De Gaulle and the birth of the Fifth Republic. Now, with the return of Mrs Gandhi, could it happen in India? How deep were the roots of India's democracy? To answer these questions, we need to retrace our steps and go back to the original constitutional settlement.

In 1946, when the Constituent Assembly began its deliberations, there was a debate about what sort of democracy would suit India. As I discussed briefly above, the overwhelming desire was for a Westminster-style democracy, which the leaders of the independence movement had been brought up to admire and emulate in their own practices. It had its dangers since it gave the elected Executive excessive powers as long as there was a majority in Lok Sabha. But people also wondered if a Western-style model would suit India's conditions with illiteracy, castes and communalism, multiple languages and religions, many regions with gross inequalities and a divisive history. Would democracy be an elite privilege, especially as the debates at first were conducted in English?

Gandhi thought that the path chosen was wrong. He wanted the Congress to disband itself as a political movement and become a vehicle for constructive work in the villages. He favoured an indirect democracy wherein villages would have their own elected panchayats and then send someone to a central body. The Centre was to be weak and power was to be devolved downwards.

The Gandhian model was rejected, as was his idea that India should be a republic of villages. The thrust of Indian policy was to be modernization via industrialization and a consequent urbanization. But even within this model, there were alternatives which had to be rejected. Thus, the model favoured by the Communist Party of India – the Soviet constitution of 1935 – was also cast aside. Apart from anything else, this model would have recognized the separate states as autonomous republics but part of the overall federation. The reality in the USSR was much more centralist than the federalist model of its constitution. The Indian leadership was haunted by the twin dangers of a weak central authority, which in its view made India liable to foreign invasion, and the balkanization of the country, especially having just been through the Partition. So it chose neither a highly decentralized Gandhian republic nor a union of autonomous republics. The Indian Union was to be quasi-federal in character with strong powers vested with the Centre.

In the first thirty years, the system displayed many of its virtues and defects. The majority enjoyed by the Congress at the Centre and in most of the states gave the initial years a stability which was necessary. There was a concordance between the Centre and the states about legislation and about economic policy. But when there was a disagreement, the Centre could wield its clout. For instance, the first elected Communist government in Kerala was dismissed on a flimsy pretext by the Centre. The imposition of President's rule became more widespread as the governments in the states took a different political hue from the Congress at the Centre after 1967. All this was a continuation of the British Raj, where the governor general used to have extensive powers over the provinces and the viceroy could dismiss rulers of native states where disorder was likely to break out. It could even be argued that the British learned their behaviour from what they saw as the Mughal imperial model of governing India.

There were two forces which saved the polity from being totally centralized. One, of course, was the fact that the judiciary, although appointed by the Executive, was by tradition and practice independent. The states could always appeal against a Central decision to the Supreme Court. In this respect, the Westminster Constitution was modified by being a written one and hence the supreme arbiter. It was the decision of the judiciary in the election case against Mrs Gandhi which went against her and caused her to resort to an Emergency. This was the only way within the Constitution for her to avoid resignation. Mrs Gandhi sought to intimidate the judiciary during the Emergency by exercising her powers to transfer judges but that did not dent its independent habits.

The other much more powerful force was the fissiparous tendency within the Congress. Inasmuch as it brought together diverse factions, it also fell foul of their desire for self-assertion, especially that of the ambitious regional satraps who represented some of these factions. By the last years of Nehru's reign, these regional leaders – Kamaraj from Tamil Nadu, Atulya Ghosh from West Bengal, S.K.Patil from Maharashtra, Nijalingappa from Karnataka and Sanjiva Reddy from Andhra Pradesh, among others, collectively known as the Syndicate – represented a new wave in Indian politics. Unlike the first generation of leaders, many of whom had been educated in Britain and discoursed in English, these men were happier speaking their regional language. Their ambitions were to control their regional base and bring American style pork barrel to it. This Syndicate chose Indira Gandhi as Shastri's successor. But the party split into two, each faction called itself Congress and could only be distinguished by its leader's name. Thus a once great party was now two – Congress (Indira) and Congress (Nijalingappa).

During the Emergency, the Congress (Indira) split further when Jagjivan Ram, the Dalit face of Congress, walked out and joined the opposition (though he returned later). Whatever the size of her majority in the Lok Sabha, Indira Gandhi had to listen to the satraps when she returned in 1980. She had no hope of returning from her old seat in Uttar Pradesh and had to contest from Andhra Pradesh. The regional power-base of the Congress was changing and that meant making new alliances within the Congress for her to stay at the top. Under her father's leadership, the Congress was a pyramid; now it was more like a multi-tiered cake. This was more akin to the classical model of Hindu kingship where the Emperor – the Chakravartin – was more a super-feudatory power, receiving homage from lesser kings and obligated to them in return as a protector, than a European-style power ruling directly.

The fissiparous tendency of the Congress is in some ways typical of Indian society. The Hindu social structure is a honeycomb of divisions and subdivisions carefully ordered by hierarchical status yet constantly shifting and adapting in the light of new developments. Thus jatis have moved up in social ranking as a result of modernization or by acquiring a higher-caste lifestyle, following a new spiritual trend or in some cases by migration. Hindus as a rule have never been a single monolithic people, though that was what haunted Jinnah. The Hindu tendency towards divisions and hierarchy infected other groups. Thus there are jati divisions among Indian Muslims as well as Christians and even Parsees. But the divisions are also fluid. One's identity can be at a family level or jati level; but at times people combine at a higher level by displaying their varna identity. Therefore, if your jati is a subcaste of the Brahmin varna, then you can join a larger group. It will depend whether in your region it is a good political strategy to display a Brahmin identity or whether even among the Brahmins there are antagonistic divisions. Thus alliances form and are broken up as electoral advantage goes one way or another. In this manner, the size of a vote bank is fluid and depends upon the arts of political mobilization that a leader can demonstrate.

The largest group is of course a linguistic or a religious group. Given India's size in terms of area as well as population, some of the linguistic groups are the size of nations. In Indian political life, especially after the trauma of Partition, there has been a reluctance to call linguistic groups 'nations'. But in effect that is what they are. Just as East Pakistan emerged as a separate nation – Bangladesh – based on language and territory, India is also full of potential nations. The federal nature of the Constitution, however, does not give too much autonomy to regions. The preservation of territorial integrity has been a first duty of all Indian governments. Thus sub-nationalisms may flourish but there are limits to how far they can go. Indian democracy has been inclusive of much diversity but one limit it has imposed is that no sub-nationality can assert independence from India. This limit was sorely tested when Mrs Gandhi returned to power in 1980.

It was during the course of Mrs Gandhi's sojourn in opposition that she had encouraged a Sikh militant leader, Sant Bhindranwale, who was demanding a separate Sikh nation – Khalistan. This was her way of weakening the Janata government. But she was playing with fire. When she returned to power, she faced the most serious separatist movement India had seen since Independence. Neither Telangana in 1948 nor Naxalbari in 1968 had been anywhere near as serious a challenge to the territorial integrity of India as Khalistan threatened to be. The dissident movement was allegedly well financed by the Sikh diaspora and its combination of religious fervour and Sikh nationalism was potent. There was also the fact that Punjab was located on the border with Pakistan. This gave rise to all the paranoia that the Indian polity is capable of. The struggle led to a serious confrontation between the Indian Army and Khalistan fighters. Punjab, a prosperous part of India, was plunged into a warlike situation and had to be 'pacified' for years after the Army attacked the holiest shrine of Sikhism – the Golden Temple in Amritsar. It cost Indira Gandhi her life when her own Sikh bodyguards killed her in her own garden in 1984. Her death unleashed a brief but bloody pogrom against the Sikhs in Delhi whose culprits remain to be punished twenty years later.

But if the Sikh nationalist movement over-reached itself, other identities asserting themselves affected politics in a more lasting way. Electoral arithmetic in terms of 'vote banks' developed in a complex form whereby identifiable collectivities – jatis, religious minorities, linguistic or regional groups – could be appealed to through their leaders or agents to cast their vote for one party rather than another. For her return to power in 1980, Mrs Gandhi manipulated the Muslim vote bank and the Dalit vote bank. While holding on to her upper caste Hindu vote bank in north India, she joined forces with the anti-Brahmin forces in south India. But then she was a national leader and held in her portfolio more than one vote bank. Others were much more local in their following, much more single vote-bank leaders, such as Charan Singh who had briefly been prime minister in the Janata government and represented the Jat farmers of north India. This was one of the early caste factions. Later still, the castes just below the upper castes – backward castes and other backward castes, formed vote banks.

The pattern of these vote banks differed according to regions. Thus it was, for example, Kammas and Reddies in Andhra Pradesh, Patidars and Kshatriyas in Gujarat, Marathas in Maharashtra, Yadavs in Uttar Pradesh and Bihar. There were Muslim vote banks in Uttar Pradesh and Bihar, which were loyal to the Congress but being wooed by other parties. At the level of general elections for the Centre, ideology and class politics still had a role in the 1980s. But state-level elections became battles for vote banks in the most blatant manner possible.

One way of viewing this development is as an aberration. The model of a liberal democracy assumes autonomous individual citizens rationally voting after balanced consideration of options available. Perhaps this could be true in an ideal world. But individuals are guided by self-interest and loyalties which exist in all societies, be they class loyalties or group, tribe or caste loyalties. The model liberal democrat was always a mythical entity. Self-interest displays itself in democratic politics in any effective way it can. Democracy in India had now settled down to a cosy accommodation with the local society, with its caste hierarchies, religious groupings and regional diversities.

This 'deepening' of Indian democracy happened because of a parallel failure on the economic front. For the first thirty years after Independence, Congress under Nehru followed a statist, capital-intensive development programme as much for national pride as for economic betterment. Growth was sluggish – about 1 to 1.5 per cent per annum per capita – labelled the 'Hindu' rate of growth. Employment failed to grow in the private sector and only public sector jobs were a booming area. The first in the queue for these public sector jobs were of course the upper caste, upper class beneficiaries of higher education at home or abroad. The lower castes, even after gaining higher education, could not enter public sector jobs till they were able to use political muscle to jump the queue. Communities used their vote banks to capture a share of power and patronage at provincial levels to grab public sector jobs.

Soon there arose a cry for positive discrimination for scheduled castes (scheduled that is in the Government of India Act of 1935) – or Dalits as they now labelled themselves. Then backward castes and the so-called other backward castes or OBCs won official listing. A report was prepared by a commission under the chairmanship of B.P. Mandal – hence the Mandal Commission – which proposed statutory reservations for Dalits and OBCs in public sector jobs and admissions to institutions of higher education. The report was shelved during the 1980s while Congress enjoyed a majority in Lok Sabha. But it was to come back to haunt Indian political parties.

The Congress majority in 1980 was more a result of the incompetence and falling out among the partners in the Janata coalition than any positive new message or even remorse at Indira Gandhi's arbitrary behaviour. The majority was strengthened when, after her tragic assassination, her son Rajiv Gandhi called an election. But both these majorities hid for a while the structural fragmentation of India's ruling party. Congress no longer had the hegemony in politics that it had enjoyed in the 1950s and even to some extent in the 1960s. Its capacity to keep together disparate interest groups had eroded. Mrs Gandhi's style of leadership was to concentrate all power in her hands. The widespread organizational structure, used to periodic elections, was neglected and elections ceased to matter in the party. Instead, it was the currying of personal favour with the leader which changed Congress culture from a democratic to a sycophantic, semi-royal one. While Mrs Gandhi lived, she could manipulate the multiple conflicts which were afoot. But after her death, the decay of the Congress became inevitable. It was only a matter of time before it sank into disrepair. But the shrinking of its power was much quicker.

At the state level, at first, its monopoly of power was challenged by smaller parties which could come together on an anti-Congress platform. This began in 1967 and continued through the 1970s at this level. Specialist parties had grown up representing a particular jati or regional interests. Dalits, Muslims, Jats, Yadavs and Patidars challenged the Congress in their strong areas. Despite the majorities of the 1980s, the Congress system had ended. Rajiv Gandhi failed to get a majority in the 1989 election and chose not to form a coalition with smaller parties. He hoped that he would soon return at the head of a Congress majority government. So he chose to support the Janata Dal government of V.P. Singh from outside. In doing so, he helped to inaugurate a new era in Indian politics. It is this era which will now be the focus of our attention.

fragmentation and inclusion

What happened after Rajiv Gandhi's defeat was a dramatic change in Indian politics. In a sense, the victory of Janata in 1977 had given a foretaste of what was to come. But, as I have argued above, the two victories of Congress under the Gandhi mother and son misled many observers. The system had fragmented into multiple parties, each representing a slice of the electorate, as against the Congress holding together many slices of the electorate within its own control.

Very few parties had national appeal. Indeed, as of 1989, Congress was the only truly national party. The two Communist parties had national aspirations but only regional presence. The Bharatiya Janata Party (BJP hereafter) had not as yet emerged in its full power. It had been helped by the Emergency and had steadily conducted a quiet cultural campaign against what it called the pseudo-secularism of the Congress. But few were prepared for the explosive electoral growth of the BJP, so that by the end of the 1990s the BJP was the alternative to the Congress as a national party.

But before that was to occur, there was a succession of coalition governments. The first of these coalition governments was led by V.P. Singh, who had been finance minister under Rajiv Gandhi but quit as a protest against the allegations of corruption connected with a defence contract awarded to the Swedish firm, Bofors. His Janata Dal was to split and spawn many similar forms as the 1990s progressed – after he was briefly prime minister. During his tenure, he implemented the recommendations of the Mandal Commission and unleashed a war of the upper castes against the backward and other backward castes (OBCs), which was to shape Indian electoral politics. The OBC wave was to stay and every party had to either include OBC candidates within its portfolio of election candidates or ensure that it could win despite the OBCs. Given the regional variations in the mix of specific OBCs, many states were to spawn an OBC party or two.

It has to be repeated that this fragmentation of parties by caste and regional cleavages was in a sense a healthy phenomenon. It meant that India's democracy had been able to include those previously denied access to power since time immemorial. Independent India failed to reform the social structure of Hindu and Muslim societies; indeed, it chose not to reform. But the backward castes were able to exploit the ballot box to upgrade themselves. Democratic politics with no single party dominance provided the perfect roulette wheel for different factions to have a go at holding office and diverting the state revenues to the advantage of their own clients. Economic dirigisme and slow growth had validated this grab of office to accelerate group mobility. But it was this dirigisme that ran the economy into the ground in 1991.

Mrs Gandhi had begun a relaxation of the self-imposed constraints of the old development model that India had adopted under Nehru. She allowed foreign borrowing, at first from the IMF and then from the Indian diaspora, i.e. the Non Resident Indians (NRIs), as well as foreign commercial banks. The economic growth rate increased from around 3.5 to 5.5 per cent and as population growth had slowed down per capita incomes began to grow at a respectable rate of 3.5/4.0 per cent during the 1980s. But the debt incurred abroad had not led to a restructuring of the economy or any marked increase in export performance. Soon the strategy ran aground. The opening of hostilities in Iraq after its invasion of Kuwait increased oil prices and stemmed the flow of remittances from the Middle East on which India had come to rely for financing its trade deficit.

In 1991 India was on the brink of a debt default. Extreme measures, such as the pledging of its gold reserves to raise loans and promises of drastic economic reform, had to be taken. The then ruling coalition under prime minister Chandra Shekhar ran out of steam and elections had to be called in early 1991. India then suffered a second assassination of a Congress leader, when Rajiv Gandhi died of a suicide bomb attack in the middle of the election campaign. In the sympathy wave which followed, Congress benefited, but even then did not win an outright majority. However, the Congress government under P.V. Narasimha Rao lasted a full five years (unlike the two previous governments of Singh and Chandra Shekhar), despite the lack of a majority. It initiated drastic reforms of the economy and the gradual abandonment of the old dirigiste model in favour of a liberal, market-oriented approach.

Given the fragility of the government, the reform process had to be consensual and hence slow. But after a bad year in which growth fell to just one per cent, the economy revived and reached a higher plateau of 6 to 6.5 per cent growth rate of GDP. India's federal system was also loosening up and this gave the governments in individual states the opportunity to run their own reform programmes at a speed different from that at the Centre. But at the state level, as at the Centre, fragile governments had to bribe their partners and detractors to stay in power, and this meant that the fiscal discipline of the first thirty years after Independence gave way to a persistent deficit. Interest groups had learnt to organize to register their demands through party factions and obtain satisfaction. Farmers got subsidized water, fertilisers and power, while enjoying generous price support for their output. Politicians went on loan *melas*, where they gave away cheap bank credit from the public sector banks.

The paradox of the 1990s is that even as the economy was put on a reform path, old style politics continued, relying on the public finances to accommodate sectional demands. Successive governments promised to tackle the budget deficit at the Centre but with little lasting success. The extra growth made the inefficiencies of pork barrel politics that much more affordable. Liberalization also brought in small amounts of foreign portfolio and direct investment. Privatization of the public sector enterprises, cautiously attempted, opened up new money for patronage.

To this heady mixture was added an uneasy marriage between politics and crime. There had been for some time a growth of the 'black' economy, which avoided tax and foreign exchange regulations. Smuggling and a foreign exchange black market had existed throughout the previous twenty years.

Politicians were always looking for ways of financing elections and they brokered a cosy partnership with criminals. Since going to prison had been respectable during the Independence struggle, the laws were lax against people with a record of imprisonment contesting elections, even when they had criminal cases outstanding or even criminal convictions in their past. Soon the law was in bed with the criminal, as the politician compromised the police under his command. If India's politics was becoming inclusive, this was an embrace too far.

But at this juncture in the early 90s, one of the oldest cleavages in Indian society was harnessed for its political uplift by the BJP. Lal Krishna Advani, the president of the BJP, chose to go on a mass mobilization drive, campaigning to build a temple on the site of the disused Babri mosque in Ayodhya. It was argued that the mosque stood on the very site where Lord Rama, the hero of the epic Ramayana and an avatar of Lord Vishnu, was born. The claim had slim foundations in history and more in mythology, but rhetorically it had a powerful appeal. The mosque was indeed dismantled on 6 December 1992, soon after the climax of Advani's rath yatra. Its destruction led to Hindu-Muslim riots across India and gave a great boost to the BJP's recruitment drive. Arguing that India was a Hindu nation and that the Constitution ought to reflect this fact, the BJP launched a Hindutva movement for electoral success.

This populist move on part of the BJP and its associated organizations collectively known as the parivar (family) led to some sharp repercussions. Communal riots between Hindus and Muslims had flared up following the declaration of a Black Day by Jinnah on 16 August 1946 and continued for the next twelve months till Independence and were a factor in the decision to partition India. But during the seventeen years of Nehru's premiership, there were hardly any such riots. After Nehru's demise there began a steady trickle of such riots but even then they were episodic rather than endemic. The three months following the destruction of the Babri mosque witnessed a large increase in incidents of communal riots. The Hindutva parivar blamed Muslims and insinuated that they were egged on by Pakistan to indulge in riotous behaviour. The revival of Hindu-Muslim riots as an endemic phenomenon is one of India's primordial fears. Suddenly it seemed that after forty-five years of a secular existence, India was about to lurch into a religious Armageddon.

If the 1960s and 1970s saw anti-Congressism as a political programme on the part of the smaller parties, the 1990s saw anti-BJP-ism as a programme. Suddenly it was the 'secular' parties which had to come together to stem the BJP tide. But some parties were against both the Congress and the BJP. This double negative lent a volatility to politics which was new.

And so, if in the first forty-two years after Independence, India had seen only six prime ministers (excluding Gulzari Lal Nanda who was interim PM for a few days twice while Congress chose a successor), in the next ten years, there were equally six prime ministers. After Rao lost the 1996 election, no single party commanded a majority. The BJP increased its seats to 180 but could not form a government that was viable. The Congress refused to get into a coalition and let a coalition of smaller parties, the United Front (a so-called Third Force), form a government. In two years, there were two prime ministers, Deve Gowda and I.K. Gujral. After elections in 1998, the BJP was able to form a coalition government but this was challenged within a year and in 1999, after yet more polls, the BJP returned to office at the head of another coalition. This NDA coalition lasted five years.

Thus, after a decade of turmoil since the defeat of Rajiv Gandhi in 1989 and the end of Congress dominance, India was back to a semblance of stability. Of course no single party commanded a majority. But at the intersection between anti-Congressism and anti-BJP-ism, enough partners were found by the BJP to allow it to govern for five years. The coalition was such that the BJP could not pursue an unadulterated Hindutva programme. Indeed, apart from its attempt to change school textbooks on history and its storming of the cultural citadels of Congress hegemony, the BJP conducted itself much like a centrist party. It pursued economic reforms, much to the chagrin of its core supporters, who were hoping for a swadeshi-autarkic-policy. But wisdom prevailed and the BJP learned to live with globalization.

The response of the Indian polity to the advent of globalization and the shock of near bankruptcy in 1991 was confused by the phenomenon of the rise of the BJP as a major force. For the first time in forty-five years, the Congress had a plausible rival party of a national stature to challenge its hegemony. As far as the economic policy arena was concerned, the battle lines were drawn according to liberalizers versus the nationalists. The liberalizers wanted to reduce state control over industrial investment, to encourage entry of foreign goods and foreign investment, to deregulate markets and replace the administrative governance of the economy by a market-based alternative. This was a reversal of the Nehru policy of planning with a predominance of state control. It was once a proud policy of the Congress, based on a strong sense of nationalism and economic xenophobia. Most other parties, with the solitary exception of the Swatantra Party, which by the 1990s had become defunct, went along with that policy. The BJP, though known as the small traders party, supported it more from a nationalist angle than a socialist one.

Since the change happened under a Congress government, there was unease both within and outside the Congress. There had been unease when Indira Gandhi, on returning to power, had taken a large loan from the IMF to help India tide over the second oil shock. But this was a much bolder step towards a market-oriented policy. Given its origins in the Bretton Woods institutions, the policy was based on what is known as the Washington Consensus. India had to go cap in hand to stave off bankruptcy and in return, it promised reforms. As the 1990s progressed, economic reform became a major pole of contention in the Indian polity.

The Congress was divided but stayed with reform while in office between 1991 and 1996. The Communist Left was, of course, anti-reform, as was the RSS, the para-military progenitor of the BJP. But the Red and the saffron forces could not combine because of another line of division. This was between the secular parties and the religious Hindu Right. The Congress and the Left and many of the regional parties were 'secular', even though they cultivated caste vote banks. Thus the two Yadav leaders in UP and Bihar – Mulayam Singh and Laloo Prasad – respectively claim to be secular but are caste based. As is the BSP – a Dalit party under Kanshi Ram and Mayawati – which has ruled UP off and on. These secular parties are agnostic about economic reform but prefer to widen state patronage for their client groups.

Yet there are other parties, such as the Samata Party of George Fernandes, which, while stoutly anti-caste, was sufficiently anti-Congress to align with the BJP during the 1999-2004 coalition. A party such as the DMK from Tamil Nadu, while anti-Brahmin in its origin, joined the NDA coalition. Its arch-rival, the AIADMK, was wooed by the BJP in the run up to the 2004 election, as it abandoned the DMK. These alliances were not based on ideology but were marriages of convenience or based on the adage that 'my enemy's enemy is my friend'.

These multiple factions divided across caste, class, regional and religious lines generate volatility in national politics but they also give scope for inclusive coalition building. The two national parties – the Congress and the BJP – have to seek local partners to make up for gaps in their caste and regional portfolio. In this search, electoral considerations dominate to an embarrassing degree.

But Indian politics also has a strong federal dimension. Whatever the intentions of the founding fathers, the outcome has been greater power to the states over the years, although the formal arrangements have not changed. The allocation of resources across the federation is determined formally by a quinquennial finance commission but actually by the state of the coalition at the Centre. The Centre has disproportionate taxing powers and thus the states depend on it for largesse. In the old days of single party dominance, these allocations were decided within the rational framework of the five-year plan and the Centre could dictate its terms. Politics filtered through the Congress Party to modify the rational allocation in the light of provincial strength. But since single party dominance went at the Centre as well as at the state level, the question of financial sharing of resources has been totally along political lines. It all depends on how strong the Central government is, what its party composition is and how those parties have fared at the state level.

Furthermore, since the timetable for general elections and elections at the state level is not uniform, India has witnessed a constant cycle of elections through the years. Thus any coalition in power is being subjected to scrutiny in one state or another, where one of the partners is facing elections. The national outcome is often a complex amalgam of state level outcomes and the mix of coalitions.

This is what makes the 2004 election result so fascinating. The NDA government, led by the BJP, had every reason to believe it would be returned to power. The economy had been doing well during 2003-04 with an 8 per cent growth rate; foreign exchange reserves were high and inflation was low. The Congress was not ready with a viable coalition at the time of election, though it had gathered some partners. Yet when the results came in, the NDA coalition lost and the Congress was able to knit together a coalition which could govern with support from the Left parties from outside the government. How had this happened and what were the explanations?

The Congress got 145 seats, while a majority requires 273. The BJP fell from 182 to 138 seats. But more than the BJP, it was its partners that suffered losses. Its partner, the Telugu Desam Party, which was ruling in Andhra Pradesh, suffered a loss due to what is called the anti-incumbency factor. Similarly, since the BJP had switched horses in midstream in Tamil Nadu, abandoned the DMK and recruited the ruling AIADMK, here again the anti-incumbency factor told against it. The Congress also suffered from anti-incumbency since its government in Karnataka lost. In these cases, except for Tamil Nadu, there were state-level elections as well as the general election simultaneously. However, this may not have made much difference. The Congress kept its share in Maharashtra in the face of incumbency and increased its share in Gujarat where the incumbent government is BJP, though there were no state assembly elections in these cases.

In the event, the Congress was able to form a coalition which gave it 222 seats and the Left parties, which had 61 seats, promised to support the coalition from the outside. Thus the Congress-led United Progressive Alliance (UPA) was able to take office in May 2004. This was a cataclysmic change for India and the world. The news that the Left was to support the UPA coalition caused a large fall on the Mumbai Stock Exchange. It recovered when it turned out that Manmohan Singh, one of the architects of the 1991-96 reforms, was to become prime minister. Yet the turnaround needed an explanation. How could the NDA lose and how did the Congress revive itself?

Of course there were broader, more macro explanations. Thus, one interpretation was that the coalition lost because the benefits of reform had been narrowly bestowed on the urban middle classes and while its slogan was 'India Shining', the common people – aam janata – had not seen any shine in their lives. The rural areas had suffered relatively, it was argued, while urban areas, especially the metropolitan areas of Mumbai, Delhi and Kolkata, had gained.

Others thought that this was a defeat for Hindutva and a triumph for secularism. The events of 1992 and the Babri mosque had an echo ten years later. The movement to build a Ram temple on the site of the mosque had been frustrated. But there had been a constant trail of volunteers – kaar sevaks – who had gone to Ayodhya to help build elements of the structure, which was to be hopefully set up. Throughout the tenure of the NDA coalition, efforts were made by the parivar parties to force the government to give the go-ahead to build the temple. But the other partners in the coalition were against any such idea, since it validated the act of vandalism which destroyed the mosque. It was the return of a group of kaar sevaks from Ayodhya to Ahmedabad that caused a crisis. On its way the train stopped at Godhra and soon afterwards a fire broke out in the compartment carrying the volunteers and burned them to death. Local Muslims were immediately blamed. This led to four days of communal riots in Gujarat. Muslims died in much greater numbers than Hindus.

The police is alleged to have connived in the attacks upon the Muslims. It was said that the Gujarat government, under BJP domination and led by Narendra Modi, who had cultivated an aggressive Hindutva image, was responsible for the breakdown of law and order. The riots stopped after four days when the army sent out from Delhi arrived and took charge. Details remain contentious and the law courts are dealing with the aftermath of the riots. Despite this development, Narendra Modi and the BJP won the state level elections later in 2002. This notwithstanding, it was felt that the losses of BJP in the Gujarat Lok Sabha seats were due to the aftermath of the riots.

There is no single explanation of the result any more than there is a single theory of any complex event. The miracle is that there was once again an orderly transfer of power. When the BJP first emerged as a party that could possibly come to power, various of its detractors raised the spectre of fascism and insinuated that once in power, the BJP might be difficult to remove. The analogy with fascist parties in Europe is unwarranted of course but the imagery is powerful. What happened in May 2004 showed that the BJP, like any other party in India, is schooled in democratic practice.

The fifteen years since the defeat of Congress under Rajiv Gandhi have led to some innovations in Indian politics. Thus a single-party majority government now seems impossible. Coalition governments, far from being an exception, are now the rule. The first two coalitions after 1989 were fragile and short-lived, as were the two after the defeat of the Congress in 1996. All these coalitions had one thing in common. They had neither of the two big national parties – the Congress or the BJP – as their members. Between 1991 and 1996, the Congress did not have an absolute majority and was about 40 seats short. Yet it could manage by manipulating the divisions within the opposition. The NDA coalition was effective, as it had more than 300 seats in the Lok Sabha, of which the principal partner, BJP, had 182. This coalition lasted a full five years. But it also needed a new element in governance. Thus, there was a cabinet with a prime minister at its head, as usual. But the coalition itself needed looking after. George Fernandes, the leader of the Samata Party, a member of the coalition, became the convenor of the NDA coalition. This was where inter-party, intra-governmental conflicts had to be resolved and the coalition had to arrive at a single view on major issues of policy. Since the coalition brought together partners with sharp ideological differences, the convenor was an alternative but complementary focus of leadership.

The incoming United Progressive Alliance (UPA) coalition has institutionalized this arrangement. Sonia Gandhi, the leader of the Congress, was expected to be prime minister, as was her right as leader of the largest faction in the coalition. But she forebore to take the office, partly sensitive about her own foreign birth and partly to wrong-foot the loud opposition to her taking the job. The prime minister is thus not the leader of the largest party in the coalition but one of her own chosen Congress members. Dr Manmohan Singh had been finance minister in the 1991 Rao government and was crucial in initiating the reforms. Then he had been brought in as a technocrat. Now he is prime minister as a Congress politician in his own right. Sonia Gandhi is the convenor of the UPA coalition and thus has the responsibility of fixing the political deals, which keeps the coalition together, while the prime minister is the chief executive of the government. It is an innovation which is still not fully embedded but even so it illustrates the capacity of the system to adjust and adapt to changing circumstances.

It is difficult to say at this juncture whether the UPA coalition will survive the full five years. Looking at the two five-year governments since 1989, that of Rao and Vajpayee, we see that they had one thing in common: the ruling or dominant party had two-thirds of the required 273 seats or more. Four other coalition governments – those of Singh, Chandra Shekhar, Deve Gowda and Gujral – did not satisfy this criterion. It is impossible to generalize from a small sample of six cases, but it makes sense that the dominant party's clout will be a function of how dependent it is on its coalition partners. In the case of the UPA coalition, its total strength falls short of 273 seats; it is the Left with its 61 seats, which is giving support from the outside, which takes the numbers above the required 273. The fault line running across the broader coalition is about economic reform while the cementing glue is that of anti-BJP-ism or secularism.

What is certain, however, is that if the present government does not last the full five years, there will be another election. This election will be fairly conducted and most likely a new coalition government will emerge. In the 1950s, since its friends feared for the health of the Indian polity post-Nehru, India was always being asked: 'After Nehru Who?' Now there is no anxiety as to whether India's democracy is here to stay. If Dr Manmohan

Singh's government were to be defeated in a no-confidence vote, there would no doubt be another government, with either himself, another Congress politician or some BJP or smaller party political leader as prime minister. India's democracy can be described by the adaptation of the old royalist slogan: the Coalition is defeated; elect a new Coalition.

warts and beauty spots

What then are the strong and weak points of Indian democracy – its beauty spots and its warts?

Its principal strong point must be its survival for a long period of time. At fifty-eight years, Indian democracy is one of the longer living and older democracies in the world. The first Indian republic has lasted longer than any of the five French republics, except the Third; longer than the inter-war German Weimar and the Austrian republics, or the Spanish republic that was destroyed in the civil war. It has done this while preserving India's territorial integrity and with only one short episode of a (constitutionally sanctioned) suspension of the basic freedoms.

The key to its survival has been its inclusiveness. The revolutionary decision of the Constituent Assembly to adopt universal adult franchise has helped Indian society to unleash the demands for inclusion from lower and backward castes and Dalits, and from marginalized groups everywhere in the country. Given the failure of successive governments to tackle root and branch reform of Hindu social structures, and indeed the consequent valorization of caste differences, political democracy has offered an alternative outlet for the ritually lower social groups to assert their strength of numbers and translate such strength into voting power. In some parts of India, south of the Vindhyas, the old Brahminical order no longer holds sway. In states such as Bihar and Uttar Pradesh, there is a constant challenge of the backward castes to the upper castes in the political arena, which often leads to violent retaliation on the part of the old elites.

This has been accomplished via a vast learning experiment in which a traditional society has taught itself modern methods of protest and mobilization, of party formation and electoral activity. The understanding of the minutiae of political factions and their provenance that the average illiterate elector has is startling. She faces being bribed and cajoled by rival parties competing for the same vote banks and has to decide for whom to cast her vote. The ways in which the Indian elector has done so continues to baffle the professional politician. The Indian voter has learnt to throw out incumbent governments at the state level on a routine basis and while the results of the latest general election may have surprised the professional commentators, the Indian elector has failed to re-elect a sitting government at the Centre in every election since 1989, with a solitary exception in 1999. This was when the BJP, after one year in office, lost a confidence vote but came back to power. This was a minor exception to the rule of anti-incumbency. In terms of voter turnout, in India, unlike in many Western countries, there is a greater willingness to vote among the lower income groups than the upper ones. The voter does not have faith in any single party but she does believe in the democratic system. The confidence that the founding fathers placed in the people of India has been vindicated.

But these achievements have been bought at a price. It is arguable that while the slow growth in per capita income in the first thirty years after Independence was probably a result of well meant but misguided economic policies, in the last twenty-five years India has been held back as the price of political fragmentation. Governments have had to maintain fragile coalitions and pacify competing vote banks by extending uneconomic, often regressive, subsidies, which lead to persistent budget deficits and a growth rate slower than what could otherwise be achieved. The recorded deficits at the Centre and in the states amount to 10 per cent of GDP. This is mainly consumption rather than investment. If invested, such a large sum would give between two and three percentage points extra growth. There has thus been a trade-off between growth and inclusion. The process of inclusion has brought lower caste and lower-class groups into power but the benefits of this empowerment have been reaped by the leaders of such groups and not flowed down to the poorest. India's efforts at poverty eradication have therefore been hampered. In terms of the head count of the poor, India fares worse than Pakistan for instance.[5] In education as well, an upper caste/upper class bias persists, since adult literacy has been neglected relative to higher education. Thus adult literacy languishes at 61 per cent but India can proudly boast of an IT software industry that is world class, since it is well supplied by college graduates.

The fragmentation of political parties has led to unstable coalitions enjoying brief tenures of office and, sensing their short tenure, indulging in most corrupt and rapacious behaviour. Nor is longevity in power any guarantee that the well being of the people, even of the favoured vote banks, will be looked after, as the example of Bihar under the fifteen-year-long domination of Laloo Prasad Yadav shows. The full costs of the drive for political inclusion have never been measured but it has made the costs of governments high. The total annual budget deficits of the Centre and the states have resisted any attempt at reduction. Half of the annual revenue of the Central government is spent on interest payment on the public debt, itself a measure more of cumulative excessive consumption by governments than of investment.

Thus while inclusion is at one level a progressive force, its 'trickle down' effects are slow. A faster rate of growth by itself may do more for poverty alleviation. Indeed, the decline in poverty indicators, such as the headcount ratio, has come only since the Hindu rate of growth of 1 to 1.5 per cent per annum was superseded in the 1980s and 1990s when more sensible economic policies were adopted. The period of high growth (1980-2004) has been accompanied by the fragmentation of party politics but this is not a causal relationship. It is possible to argue that the growth could have been higher without the fragmentation (Desai 2004).

The brief period of authoritarian behaviour (1975-77) has other lessons to teach us about a major drawback of Indian democracy. This is the dynastic urge in the Congress Party. The Nehru-Gandhi dynasty ruled India for thirty-seven out of the first forty-two years between 1947 and 1989. Lately, the fortunes of the party have been revived by the emergence of Sonia Gandhi as the leader of the Congress, with the presence of her son Rahul as a newly elected MP and daughter Priyanka as an active Congress leader. As a party, the Congress has abandoned contested elections to its top posts and the chosen few at the top are the coterie of the Gandhi leadership. Indira Gandhi began this practice of personal rule over the party. It fell into disuse briefly after Rajiv Gandhi's assassination in 1992. Yet six years later, the party welcomed the leadership of Sonia Gandhi, his widow, with open arms.

Dynastic politics is not unique to India. Sri Lanka's President Chandrika Kumaratunga is the daughter of two prime ministers, her mother having succeeded her father after his murder. There are the Bhuttos in Pakistan and in Bangladesh the leaders of the two principal parties are a daughter and a widow of previous political leaders. Aung San Suu Kyi is the daughter of Myanmar's first leader, Aung San. Indonesia has Megawati Sukarnoputri, who recently lost the presidential elections having been president previously. Yet the longevity of the Nehru-Gandhi dynasty is something unique and cannot be healthy for a democracy.

The practice of the Congress Party in institutionalizing personal rule has spread to other political parties. The BJP reappointed Advani as the leader without an election and, with the exception of the Left parties, political parties such as Laloo

Prasad Yadav's Rashtriya Janata Dal or the Bahujan Samaj Party of Mayawati or Lok Jan Shakti Party of Ram Vilas Paswan are just personal fiefdoms. And this is not just a north Indian problem. The DMK expects that when its leader Karunanidhi retires his son Stalin would take over. The son-in-law of Andhra chief minister and Telugu film star, N.T. Rama Rao, succeeded him at the helm of the Telugu Desam Party. The fact that Chandrababu Naidu proved to be a modernizing, techno-savvy chief minister is no more relevant to the dynastic disease than the fact that he fell victim to the anti-incumbency effect at the 2004 election. The Shiv Sena leader Bal Thackeray has a son and a nephew fighting it out for succession and Amarinder Singh, a scion of the Patiala royal family, is the chief minister of Punjab. In Jammu and Kashmir, Sheikh Abdullah created his own dynasty when his son Farooq Abdullah returned from London to take over the reins of power. His son, Omar Abdullah, continues the tradition, being an MP and a former minister in the NDA government. The new chief minister of Kashmir, Mufti Mohammad, has his daughter as a minister in the government. One could go on and on.

A more serious problem is the politicization of all aspects of public life. Indira Gandhi started the trend, aided and abetted by the communist parties, of claiming that the popular mandate gave her the power to override conventions and even the Constitution. She took to transferring members of the judiciary to remoter parts of India in an attempt to browbeat them. Her attempts at land reform without compensation were thwarted by the Supreme Court in the famous Golak Nath case, which reaffirmed the right to private property enshrined in the Constitution. But the interference of the elected leader in the transfer and promotion of top civil servants and of top officers of the police are routine. Public servants in India know that they serve whosoever is the ruling chief minister and accept they have to bend the rules to suit their current masters. Occasionally, a case comes to the court bringing such practices to light.

The courts are a restraint on populist political extravagances but they are slow and overburdened with a huge backlog of cases. Justice is delayed by years if not decades. Witnesses are suborned, bribed, threatened, so that they fail to appear before the courts, or change their testimony or turn hostile. Two of the worst episodes of communal violence – the 1984 anti-Sikh riots in Delhi and the 2002 Gujarat riots – have led to no convictions thus far, despite investigations by official commissions and NGOs. The politically powerful have ways of protecting the culprits in their midst and even rewarding them with promotions and perks. The seasoned politician, when caught and perchance convicted, develops a weak heart and has to be placed in a comfortable bed in a posh hospital. If in jail, he manages to get all the comforts and privileges as befits his status. The public is aware of the identities of these people and has become cynical about the prospects of bringing them to book.

The widespread prevalence of public ownership of banks and industrial and other enterprises also leads to the extensive exercise of patronage. There are opportunities for corruption and embezzlement. Thus Laloo Prasad Yadav, when chief minister of Bihar, is alleged to have embezzled a large sum of money, running into millions of rupees, in a fodder scam. He had to give up his post, replacing himself with his wife. He has not been convicted in five years and is now a member of the Central cabinet as minister for railways, the only department with its own budget. Politics thus shelters financial crime as much as violent crime, as long as the culprit has connections.

This politicization of public life has left only the army and the judiciary as trusted public institutions in India. For the rest, the citizen's access to the goods and services provided by the state can be secured only by displaying a caste, religious or regional identity, the membership of a viable vote bank, and only through agents who deploy the vote bank at higher levels. Everything the state has touched – education at the primary, secondary and the tertiary levels, any public sector appointments, sports, medicine – has been corrupted. The few islands where merit rather than connections count such as the Indian Institutes of Technology (IITs) and of Management (IIMs) – centres of excellence in higher education – have to protect their independence jealously. The NDA government threatened the IIMs when the education minister, Murli Manohar Joshi, proposed that they subsidize the entry of 'deserving' students or face government displeasure. Only the defeat of the coalition saved the IIMs from this piece of populism. But one cannot say for how long.

Corruption has taken a democratic dimension in as much as it prevails at all levels from the bottom to the top and affects all parties. The prime minister, Dr Manmohan Singh, is specially singled out and praised for his totally clean career. Even those who so praise him do not understand that by implication all else stand indicted. There was an allegation that Rajiv Gandhi, when prime minister, awarded a defence contract to the Swedish firm Bofors in return for a large bribe. His finance minister V.P. Singh, quit the government on this issue. The case is even now dragging on after fifteen years, being taken up when a government hostile to the Congress is in power and dropped when the Congress or its allies return to office. It came to a conclusion favourable to Rajiv Gandhi recently but one cannot predict closure.

When a corruption scandal of the NDA government was exposed by an online newspaper, *Tehelka*, with video tapes, the case was never brought to court. The newspaper, on the other hand, suffered persecution and harassment, as it was suspected of being in the pay of the opposition. Now that the then opposition is in power, there will be some movement on the case, not so much to obtain justice but to settle scores.

Yet all this has taken place in the context of one of the world's freest presses and electronic media. The growth of the TV and online news channels in the last dozen years has been an astonishing phenomenon. Until the beginning of the reform process in the 1990s, there was only one TV channel – the official Doordarshan. Even the destruction of the Babri mosque was seen by Indians only on CNN since Doordarshan would not show it. Censorship was widespread and accepted. It is only liberalization which led to alternatives being available. But of course there is a nexus between big money, journalism and politics and not every journalist is independent. The size of the press, however, does matter and it can be a constant irritant to the politicians.

There is also now an active civil society pursuing public interest litigation. Human rights violations by the public authorities are exposed and pursued in the courts. India has a National Human Rights Commission to add some weight to such campaigns. There are websites which expose the crime and corruption records of parliamentarians and think tanks are busy drawing up alternative scenarios for India's polity. There are impatient young men and women who have joined the Maoists in Bihar and Andhra Pradesh fighting for the rights of the poorest in defiance of local landlords. In Kashmir, there has been an agitation since 1989. That was when the people of Kashmir began to despair of ever having a fair election without interference from Delhi. In a volatile situation, mixed up with terrorist incursions from the Pakistan and Afghanistan borders, there has grown up a vocal set of rival groups arguing for a constitutional debate about Kashmir's future. More than a decade later, there has again been a newly and fairly elected government. There is a thaw within Kashmir and a better climate of negotiations between India and Pakistan.

Democracy in India is more akin to American democracy in the era of robber barons and corrupt politicians, with its heady mixture of ethnic and immigrant groups, class cleavages as well as rural/urban and North/South divisions. It is vigorous and very much ingrained in the native culture. A country with six hundred million electors has never been seen before. India, when all is said and done, is its own invention as far as its democracy is concerned.

the future of indian democracy

It seems reasonably certain that India will continue to be a democracy for the foreseeable future. Alternative scenarios of a dictatorship or a Red Revolution can be dismissed as implausible. One can also dismiss any likelihood of a major war with China on the Himalayan border. Despite the nuclear arms parity with Pakistan, I would hazard the judgment that no major conflict will take place between the two countries. It may even be that because of the nuclear arms, any likely conflict will be prevented by American or a more international intervention. Nor is India likely to break up, as was feared for many years by the generation that lived through Partition. Khalistan was the one demand that brought India to the brink of maximal armed intervention. Kashmir remains a hot spot but is now in a better shape and nearer to some sort of resolution. The secessionist sentiments in some of the north-eastern states – Nagaland for one – are also being tackled. There will always be local subnationalist agitations, as in Assam or Telangana in Andhra Pradesh. Yet these many discontents are manageable precisely because there is a democratic framework.

In this sense, India has the anomalous property that there is no permanent majority. There is no monolithic block Hindu vote, despite the 80 per cent plus of Hindus in the population. Thus, while Jinnah feared that Muslims would be in a permanent minority position, what he missed is that the size of India and the inherent dividedness of Hindu social structures are guarantees that no single majority can be built relying on Hindus. The North differs from the South about Brahmin domination, the Dalits stand outside the structure, the backward castes resent the upper ones even when they are economically dominant as with the Patidars in Gujarat or the

Marathas in Maharashtra. India has a number of small solid vote banks, none large enough to rule on its own, each needing others to come to office, watching how the rest of the vote banks react if they are to cling on to power. It is a vindication of James Madison's analysis of American prospects in his famous federalist essay. The kaleidoscope has to be shaken continually to generate new patterns and as it turns some of the same fragments reappear in new formations.

Even so, we need to address the position of the largest minority group – the Muslims. This is partly because even after Partition, many Muslims stayed behind in India and they have made a permanent home there. While Nehru's vision and vigilance protected them from detractors, in the last twenty years there have been siren voices questioning the 'pseudo-secularism' of Congress. Can Muslims feel safe in the future in India?

Muslims are a large minority in India but it is not their share of the total population that is important. It is their strength in many local electorates – in UP, Bihar, Andhra Pradesh, Kerala – which gives them a sense of power. Where they are in a permanent minority, they combine with others to shelter within 'secular' parties. It is only episodically, in cases like Gujarat in March 2002, that the unexpected and horrible act of an officially sanctioned attack happens. If it excites disgust and protest, it is because in the fifty-five years since Independence it was the only example of official sanction for Hindu violence against Muslims.

Yet there is one question any discussion of Indian democracy's prospects must address. Is there a serious prospect of India becoming a Hindu republic rather than a secular one, as is enshrined in the Constitution? If so, what would be the position of Muslims and all the other non-Hindu minorities in such a state?

It is, in my view, unlikely that India will become a Hindu republic because of the fragmented nature of Hindu society.

Hinduism has no single book, no single priesthood, no single God. Political parties running on a religious ticket, such as the Ram Rajya Parishad and even the Jan Sangh, did not make large inroads in the Lok Sabha. It was only when the Jan Sangh took part in the popular and 'secular' agitation against Indira Gandhi's high-handed methods in the Emergency that it gained a popular base. It changed its name to the Bharatiya Janata Party and through the 1980s established a foothold in many north and western Indian states. It has never penetrated the South, nor West Bengal or the North East. Even though it has recruited more widely among the backward castes, Dalits and even Muslims, it remains an upper caste, north Indian party. It increased its number of seats to 182 in 1996 and got stuck there in 1998 and 1999. It could on its own thus reach only up to two-thirds of the required number for a bare majority. In 2004, it has fallen back to 138. Can it reverse its decline and climb back up and beyond the 182 ceiling?

The behaviour of the BJP since its defeat is a sad reflection on a once powerful party. During the 1990s, when it was increasing its mass support, its detractors feared that this indeed was the face of Indian fascism. Today, it is a querulous, disheartened, disparate party. Within its upper echelons, there is a division between those who would take the BJP further along the economic reform path which it pursued so successfully while in office – leaders such as Arun Jaitley and Pramod Mahajan – and those who think that the party betrayed its Hindutva roots and should get back to the popular platform of temple building in Ayodhya – Uma Bharti and Narendra Modi. Political parties often go through such a phase state when they lose an election unexpectedly and get thrown out of office. It happened to the British Labour Party after 1979 and is now happening to the British Conservative Party since 1997. At present, it is not clear how the BJP will get back into a winning form. Yet it is worth exploring whether this is possible.

There is a strong belief in Indian politics that only a secular polity will suit India and that any strong religious flavour to a party's programme will be ruinous. Yet the BJP has come much farther than anyone expected in the high noon of Congress domination. It is not impossible, of course, to have an official religion and still build a tolerant society. Despite its long civil war, one would not call Sri Lanka an intolerant society, although it is now officially a Buddhist state. Malaysia manages to have a high degree of racial harmony within an Islamic framework. Israel has large Arab non-Jewish population despite its theocratic bias. In Europe, there are now a number of countries which have an official religion, usually Christianity – Catholic, Orthodox Greek or Protestant. The memories of European anti-semitism are recent enough to be cautious on this account but there now seems to be tolerance of other religions or sects.

In the post-war rebuilding of Europe, Christian Democratic Parties played a major role – in Italy and Germany especially. To be able to win elections, these parties had to combine a commitment to Christianity without excluding non-Christians or downplaying their Christian character. This meant an emphasis on Christian values rather than Christian rituals. The main thrust of Christian democracy was anti Communist and hence Christian democratic parties downplayed class conflict and talked of class cooperation and of limits to the operation of the market. Thus Germany's Social Market philosophy combined a social conscience with economic efficiency.

If India is to ever be a Hindu republic, it can only achieve this along the lines of European countries. It would take a party, perhaps the BJP, to construct a social philosophy of Hinduism stripped of its inegalitarian values of caste and untouchability. It would have to be ecumenically tolerant of other religions, and indeed, within the multi-faceted nature of Hinduism, of all the variants of Hinduism itself. A Hindu party would have to be light in its religiosity and serious in its social message to be able to command a majority. In such a state, Muslims would be safe since tolerance would be at the heart of the polity. That is to say, one need not be 'secular' in the sense in which the word is used in India to be tolerant.

It is difficult to see that the BJP could meet this challenge, since its co-habitees in the parivar – the RSS, the Vishwa Hindu Parishad, the Bajrang Dal – are into a fanatical pursuit of religiosity and hatred of non-Hindu minorities, even as they celebrate the tolerant nature of Hinduism. It has to embrace its modernizers to be like the European Christian Democrats. It will have to become what the Swatantra Party tried to be – a right wing, pro-market party. It will have to go light on religion but strong on social values derived from religion. Even then, it is a moot point whether it could command a majority in the Lok Sabha on its own or even with an ally like the Shiv Sena.

In 2004, the Congress surprised everyone by winning the largest number of seats for a single party. In 1998, the Congress had gone down to 141 seats, one of its worst showings. Sonia Gandhi initiated a no-confidence vote in the Lok Sabha in early 1999. But the Congress could not amass enough allies to form an alternative government and elections were held again. The Congress then got only 112 seats. It was widely expected that if the NDA coalition were to win in 2004, it would spell the end of the Congress. However Sonia Gandhi campaigned successfully across India, a telling contrast with Vajpayee, who had health problems. The Congress victory is very much Sonia Gandhi's vindication. The question is whether this is a sign that the Congress is back on the road to becoming a majority party.

The Congress is now firmly back in its dynastic mould, which it escaped in the six years after Rajiv Gandhi's death. Sonia Gandhi is conscious of her foreign origins and therefore her hold on the Congress leadership is precarious. So her son, Rahul Gandhi, has been encouraged to enter the Lok Sabha and is being groomed for succession. Her daughter, Priyanka, was regarded as the more likely heir a few years ago but the choice has been made to push the son. Dynastic succession has its problems, however. It alienates others who may fancy their chances of the top job. Thus Sharad Pawar left Congress on the issue of Sonia's right to lead and has formed his own National Congress Party (NCP). He is now an ally of Congress but his case illustrates the fact that ambitious and able leaders may avoid the Congress knowing that the succession is sealed.

The Congress has lost its foothold in the two most populous states – UP and Bihar. These account for 120 seats in the Lok Sabha. It is competing in these states with local parties – the Samajwadi Party (SP) of Mulayam Singh Yadav and the Rashtriya Janata Dal of Laloo Prasad Yadav respectively. Rahul Gandhi is an MP from UP, as was his father and grandmother and great-grandfather. One scenario is that in the next elections in UP, the Congress could make a large dent in the SP's strength and even be at the head of a coalition government. In such a scenario, Rahul could be the chief minister and gain experience for his eventual premiership. Winning back UP with its eighty Lok Sabha seats is vital for the Congress.

The Congress has a greater reach across India than the BJP. It can win in Haryana and Punjab and has in the past taken Rajasthan and Madhya Pradesh from BJP. It is the sole opposition party in Gujarat to the BJP and has kept winning in Maharashtra in an alliance with the NCP. In Karnataka, Kerala and Andhra Pradesh it has a fighting presence. Tamil Nadu and West Bengal are the only states where it is out of the running in any serious fashion. It has allies in the states where it is not in the running – except in UP.

The Congress used to be a portmanteau party holding diverse vote banks together. But over the years, it has split many times and many smaller parties have come up specializing in specific vote banks – the Yadavs of UP and Bihar for instance. Thus the core support for the Congress has eroded. This happened suddenly in the decade after 1989. The Congress now wants to be a pro-poor party, commanding support in the rural areas. It is also a party which hopes to attract Muslim voters.

This is again possible when local 'secular' parties are not competing with it. The same is true of its appeal to Dalits, who now have the Bahujan Samaj Party (BSP), which claims their allegiance. Relative to the BJP, however, the Congress gets more Muslim and Dalit votes and fewer upper caste votes, despite its upper caste leadership.

The 2004 elections are a pointer in this respect. The Congress got 26 per cent of the popular vote and BJP 22 per cent, though the difference in seats is only seven between the two. With its nineteen allies, the Congress mustered 36.5 per cent share of the votes and 222 seats, while the BJP with its eleven allies managed 35.88 per cent of the votes and 189 seats. The Left parties got 61 seats or 8 per cent – mainly in West Bengal and Kerala. When the Left decided to support Congress, there was then a majority. The Congress would need to generate on its own at least 80 to 100 more seats to be able to rule single-handedly. It is difficult to see where it can get these seats, which parties with specific vote blocks it could absorb or permanently defeat. The fragmentation of political parties is akin to a division of labour or specialization. This makes specific parties smaller but it gives them a greater hold on their vote bank.

As a generalist, portmanteau party, the Congress lacks focus. It has no sharp ideological message, unlike the BJP. It is secular and fights for equity but in this it has rivals on the Left and in many specific parties which represent the backward castes and Dalits. A dynastic face is an advantage in terms of recognition but it is doubtful that the charisma of Nehru and his daughter, with the memories of the Independence movement still alive, can be captured by Rahul Gandhi who has taken to politics not as a vocation but as an heirloom. Yet the hope is that a party like Congress can be held together by a dynastic leader, who promises that power will be won soon, and if won kept for a long time. The Congress is clearly taking a gamble that it will build on dynasty rather than ideology. It is difficult to see how such a strategy can succeed.

A more likely prospect is that the two large national parties – the BJP and the Congress – will get a smaller share of votes and seats and the fragmentation of the political party structure will continue apace. In 2004, the two national parties polled 48.6 per cent of the vote and got 283 seats. This was respectively 3.5 per cent and 13 seats less than they managed in 1999. The Congress has seen better days and won three times as many seats as it has now. The system of first-past-the-post, in which a mere plurality is sufficient for election rather than a clear majority, favours large parties and gives them a higher share of seats than votes. In India, however, over the years this 'multiplier' has eroded, so that the Congress had a multiplier of just 1.01 and BJP one of 1.14.[6] Thus India is on a virtual proportional representation voting system. This is also a much fairer system for small parties.

The interplay of state level results with federal ones in the 2004 elections raises the possibility that there will be no large national parties in the near future. BJP is after all a north Indian party and since its heyday in the 1990s, it has shrunk in UP and Bihar. It is currently strong in Rajasthan, Madhya Pradesh, Gujarat and Maharashtra. The Congress has a wider base across India, as we saw above, absent only in Tamil Nadu and West Bengal on a permanent basis. It too has shrunk in UP and Bihar. Yet it is possible to envisage that like the BJP, the Congress will be a party with a presence in the north-western part of India, with local parties ousting it in Andhra Pradesh and Kerala. The Congress is trying to keep together an alliance of the Muslims and the rural poor and Dalits, but it has rival parties which claim a share of these vote banks. It is blamed for many of the problems India faces today.

If such is the future of Indian democracy, with only regional parties and with even the Congress and the BJP being merely multi-regional rather than national, then coalition governments will be permanent. The experience of the years since 1989 shows that coalition governments are now routinely accepted. Alliances of up to fifteen parties are not unknown. The set of parties, which are both anti-Congress and anti-BJP, constitute a 'Third Force' and have grabbed power between 1989 and 1991 and again between 1996 and 1998. But each time they needed outside support from either the Congress or the BJP. Yet if these two shrink, they will just be large rather than dominant parties. This is normal practice in some European countries – Netherlands and Belgium, for instance. No single party dominates and the office of the prime minister can rotate, as indeed it did between Deve Gowda and Gujral in the United Front governments from 1996 to 1998.

Such a scenario will be in line with the increasing inclusiveness that has characterized Indian democracy. But, as I have argued above, there are economic costs to this inclusiveness. National parties have some sense of the need for sustained GDP growth; whereas the smaller parties are more interested in distribution of the fiscal pie out of the GDP than in its growth. The need to control budget deficits is lost on smaller parties, as was demonstrated when the outgoing United Front government gave a most generous settlement on public sector pay in 1998. It was above what the Pay Commission had recommended and even more than what the public sector unions affiliated to the Left parties – which were part of the ruling coalition – had asked for. The settlement has wrecked the budgets of many states and saddled the Central budget with a substantial future burden of salaries and pensions.

It is possible that institutional arrangements can be put in place to enforce budgetary discipline. There is already legislation for fiscal responsibility in existence, which will force the Central government to reduce the deficit by 2009. If this is delivered by this government or its successor, then one can be confident that the costs of future coalition governments can be kept in check. Yet it is unlikely that coalition governments will be able to take the hard decisions that have to be taken in any growth strategy. India could settle into a moderate growth rate zone of 5 rather than 7 or 8 per cent per annum. While this is not bad, it will mean a slower pace of reduction in poverty than has been the case in the last two decades. This, however, is for the Indian people to choose.

There is another alternative which I have advocated, though it is an unlikely scenario. This is a Grand Coalition between Congress and BJP. Their divisions are no longer across the economic reform agenda. The Congress has abandoned the Nehruvian model of economic development, though its Left partners in the current government still favour it. There is still a divide along secular-communal lines. The BJP, with the exception of the Gujarat episode, behaved itself when in power, since it was kept in check by its partners. It is not unlikely that the Congress could keep the BJP's more zealous members under control. Such a government could pursue economic growth vigorously; even 8 to 9 per cent growth rate is not out of reach. This could reduce poverty at a faster rate. It could generate sufficient economic activity outside the public sector so that the pressure on the public finances can be lower. India may yet achieve prosperity as well as democracy.

Either way, India's democracy is deep and strong. It is in tune with the native social structure and it has been adapted to local customs and practices. It has accommodated the diversity across regions, languages and cultures. It speaks with local tongues yet within a Westminster framework. It has vindicated the faith the founding fathers placed in the people when they chose universal adult franchise. They had practised a version of democracy without power during the Independence movement. What they bequeathed has empowered India's majority, which had been marginalized for centuries. That is their greatest achievement.

references:

There is a vast literature on India's politics and the working of its democracy. The special election issue of *Economic* and

Political Weekly (18-24 December 2004), already cited above in the footnote in the last chapter, contains many references and is the best single guide with which to start.

I have discussed many of these issues in greater detail in Meghnad Desai (2004), *Development and Nationhood: Essays in the Political Economy of South Asia* (Delhi, Oxford University Press).

1. The Partition created two countries but India retained its pre-independence name while Pakistan was created *de novo*. I have used the label Indica for the pre-1947 undivided India in my earlier writings (Desai 2004) but avoid that here because I am mainly concerned with post-1947 India. The Constitution calls the entity 'India, that is Bharat'. Pakistan insists on calling India by its Sanskrit/Hindi name: Bharat.
2. An example of this procedural correctness was seen when as chairman of the Planning Commission he wrote a letter submitting the Plan document to the Prime Minister of India – himself. This was to clarify that while the two positions were held by him, this was neither a permanent nor an ex-officio arrangement.
3. Rajni Kothari, (1970) *Politics in India* (Delhi; Orient Longman).
4. An American political scientist Selig Harrison wrote about this in his *India:The Most Dangerous Decades*.
5. The Human Development Report 2004 gives the percentage of population with income at below $ 1 a day as 34.7 in India and 13.4 in Pakistan. Both countries have a similarly abysmal position in the Human Development Index, which measures life expectancy, education and income jointly. India was 127th and Pakistan 142nd out of 177 countries in the 2004 HDR.
6. I derive this from 'The Elusive Mandate of 2004' by Yogendra Yadav in *Economic* and *Political Weekly*, 18-24 December 2004, p.5383-98.

why pakistan is not a democracy

aitzaz ahsan

When I was asked to contribute to this volume, I was a shade apprehensive and unsure. More questions than answers rushed to mind. Perplexing questions. How would one categorize Pakistan's political system: dictatorship or democracy, liberal or fundamentalist, civil or praetorian? Was it a mix of everything, a multi-layered hybrid? Or did Pakistan have its own unique system of governance based on so-called 'constitutional' dictatorships or quasi-military rule? How else could one explain the strange combination in which authoritarian rule appeared to have existed side by side with apparent press freedoms and habeas corpus? Why also did democracy appear not to have prevailed in Pakistan as it had in India, even though both countries had inherited the same traditions from the apparently unifying administration of the same Raj? Or had they?

The questions were profound and certainly begged for answers. I was also daunted by the thought of co-authoring a volume with none other than Lord Meghnad Desai. This was like holding a faint torch to the strong blinding beam of a powerful searchlight. But the questions themselves generated such an interest in me that I braced myself for the challenge of addressing them to the best of my ability.

The fact is that India has remained a democracy all its independent years. Pakistan has not. Both had remained under the same rulers for almost a millennium. Both seemed to be common legatees of the same politico-legal system introduced by the British. Both had simultaneously attained independence. Why then was it possible for the one to take the democratic route as the other faltered and fell prey to praetorianism?

What was the cause of the initial fragility of the democratic concept in the Pakistani environment? Was it the seeming ascendancy of the fundamentalists in the political arena of Pakistan? Was Islamic culture and outlook antagonistic to democratic norms? Was democracy subverted by the dominance of the praetorian elite in the state structures of Pakistan? And if any such ascendancy and dominance have indeed been established what, more fundamentally, have been the underlying causes? Can this ascendancy and dominance be attributed to some historical experience or inherent trait of the peoples of the Indus region (which today forms Pakistan) that is different from the character of those who inhabit the Indian mainland? Or are democratic values coterminous somehow with either the India-Indus or the Hindu-Muslim divide in the subcontinent? And if so, why?

Before attempting to discern the causes of what appears to many as the failure of the democratic process in Pakistan I must put in a caveat for the reader. Let it not be assumed that in spelling out the causes I mean to justify the absence of democracy in this country. I have myself suffered long terms in jail under military and authoritarian regimes in pursuit of the democratic ideal. I cannot give up that cause. I consider democracy as the birthright of every citizen of Pakistan: a state created by the ballot and by the people's will, even while its founding was opposed both by the fundamentalist and praetorian establishments. And I have witnessed, at first hand, the widespread demonstration of Pakistani citizens' commitment to the democratic ideal, raising slogans of hope and a better tomorrow, even as they were charged by military personnel, flogged in public, incarcerated without trials, tried summarily by military courts, even hanged after arbitrary mistrials, denying due process. The intent here is thus not to justify authoritarianism, but to probe its causes to enable a redressal and removal of those causes themselves.

One fact is undeniable. There has been a frequent denial of democracy in Pakistan. Four prolonged military regimes headed by army chiefs, have spanned thirty-three of our fifty-seven years as an independent state. Additionally, the constant intervention by the army chiefs and the GHQ in the political affairs at all other times has undermined democratic structures in Pakistan. Why was Pakistan, which apparently shared the same political and military traditions with India, not able to subordinate its military commanders to civil democratic institutions?

I have divided this essay into two parts: the first about events preceding Partition and the second about developments after the formation of Pakistan. The second part, being obviously the longer one, is further divided into several sections highlighting the roles of the civil and military bureaucracy, the superior judiciary, the elements of civil society, and the fundamentalists. Since free and fair elections are the basis of any functioning democracy, a separate section examines briefly the process of 'election management' in Pakistan.

PART I: THE CAUSES OF PARTITION

In my view, there are some essential and primordial differences between Pakistan and India, which led to the divide called Partition. Pakistani historians attribute the impulse towards Partition only to the Hindu-Muslim communal divide while Indian historians altogether deny the reality of this divide. The truth lies somewhere in between. In fact I would argue that the two regions (the Indus region and what is now India) were, in the final analysis, torn apart as much, if not more, by distinctness of culture and economic disparities as by communal differences between Hindus and Muslims. Thus a reappraisal of the distinct and differing history of the two regions, Indus (Pakistan) and India, may perhaps provide one comprehensive answer to the various haunting questions raised above.[1]

The effect of divergence and difference of religion, dogma and ritual between the Hindus and the Muslims in the partition of the subcontinent is frequently exaggerated. Pakistani writers contrast Hindu polytheism with Islam's strident monotheism and point to causes of offence. Though several Muslim ascetics prompted some forms of devotional dance, the tantric cults of Shaivite Hinduism cause outrage amongst most fundamentalist Islamists. The Hindu practice of sati and the straitjacket of caste offended Muslim observers, though Muslim rulers did nothing to eradicate the former and, in fact, profited by a clever adoption of the latter. Muslims were also voracious eaters of beef, despite the reverence that the overwhelming majority of the subcontinent bestowed upon the cow. Idol worship was anathema to zealous Muslim iconoclasts seeking glory in the scales of Allah. However, in the historical context, Hindus have always had much more to complain about regarding the incursions of Sultan Mahmood of Ghazni, and persecution at the hands of Sultan Feroz Shah and Emperor Aurangzeb.

Despite these apparently irreconcilable causes of tension and conflict, harmonious and peaceful coexistence between the communities remained the rule rather than the exception. Though, until recently, there have been no inter-marriages on any significant scale and there still are no common places of worship, there was widespread commonality of interests and lifestyles. Over centuries, most political alliances and military campaigns cut across the communal divide. Muslim and Hindu soldiers and generals fought shoulder to shoulder against Hindu and Muslim adversaries. Hindu and Muslim ministers and generals continued to serve Muslim and Hindu rulers. The Delhi sultans and the Mughals themselves employed non-Muslims in high positions of trust in the state and the army.

Hindu and Muslim feudatories frequently entered into inter-communal alliances. This was of general occurrence, although some instances are more prominent. In 1751, when Nawab Wazir Safdar Jang of Oudh sacked the Muslim principality of Rohilkhand he could do so only with the aid of the Maratha armies of Holkar and Scindia and the Jat troops of Raja Suraj Mal. As his Muslim generals betrayed Nawab Sirajuddaula at the Battle of Plassey in 1757, the Hindu divan Ram Narain stood by him. Upon hearing of the humiliation and blinding of the Muslim emperor Shah Alam at the hands of the Muslim chieftain Ghulam Qadir Rohilla, it was the Maratha chief Scindia who ordered his general Rana Khan to rescue the blinded Muslim emperor along with the Muslim princesses of the royal blood from the clutches of their Muslim tormentor. The Muslim captor had humiliated the Muslim princesses by forcing them to dance like nautch girls. The Hindu army brought them back with the dignity, respect and deference that they expected of their subjects. On the other end of the scale, Raja Jai Singh of Amber himself arrested the elusive Hindu hero, Shivaji, and carried him a prisoner to the Muslim emperor Aurangzeb.

Even at the popular level, such Indian festivals as Holi, Dussehra, Diwali, Baisakhi and Basant were celebrated by all communities. Many Muslim kings of Delhi and emperors of India enthusiastically participated in such celebrations. They even took Hindu princesses to be their queens. Most of these ladies remained practising and devout Hindus, even after their marriages. Over time, a common form of literary expression and a common literary heritage also developed. Though initially derived from Persian tradition, such idyllic images as buth (idol), buth kada (the temple), mae (wine), maekhana (the wine shop) and saqi (the cup bearer) were freely used in the Urdu and vernacular works of Muslim poets, even when these were abhorrent in the eyes of Islamic orthodoxy. And such exclusively Islamic concepts and images as Allah, Khuda, Ka'aba, qiamat, jannat, jahannum, marqad ma'shooq became the tools of Hindu poets and writers.

Muslim sufis and followers of the Bhakti movement, commonly described as the syncretics, also played an important part in forging links and developing a spirit of coexistence between the two communities. Their message, spanning several centuries, was simple, consistent and unwavering. They pleaded for peace, harmony, love and coexistence. They spread the message of communal tolerance and roundly condemned the agents of conflict.

The Uprising of 1857 was a unique picture of doing and dying together. Both communities together entered into a life and death battle against the British. The Uprising itself had been triggered by the greased cartridges that incensed both Hindu and Muslim soldiers at the Meerut Garrison in May. The Oudh populace that rose to welcome the galloping patriots, village after village and town after town, was drawn from both communities. Indeed, from Mangal Panday to Nana Sahib, from Tantia Tope to the young Rani of Jhansi, perhaps a greater number of Hindu names come to mind, as one scans for prominent personalities in the upsurge of the Hindu-Muslim masses who rose in defence of a feeble Muslim emperor.

A commonality of cause was also evident at another and, indeed, opposing level. Even though, by and large, the Uprising was the violent reaction of the old order and values against the new, at the same time the majority of Indian princes, Hindu and Muslim, were united in giving unflinching support to the British occupiers. 'Among these, the Raja of Jind was the first man, European or Indian, to take to the field against the freedom fighters. His contingents collected supplies in advance for the English troops marching upon Delhi. The Raja was also present at the Battle of Alipur and his troops took a significant part in the final assault on Delhi in September 1857. Raja Randhir Singh of Kapurthala marched into Jullundur and held the *Doab* which was virtually denuded of British troops. He then led his men right into Oudh to suppress the Uprising. Fareedkot placed himself under the orders of the Deputy Commissioner of Ferozpur and assisted him in protecting the ferries on the river Sutlej. He also personally led the attack on the stronghold of Sham Das, an energetic revolutionary, and destroyed it. Nabha held the city of Ludhiana for the British and helped in suppressing the Jullundur insurgency at Phillaur[2]. Neither Islamic nor Hindu persuasions had motivated the princes. Only perceived self-interest had moved them to stand by the new imperial power.

Communal coexistence did, of course, break down at times. There were occasional conflicts, sometimes quite gory. But the periods of harmonious coexistence were far more extended than the episodes of conflict. And when any such conflict did take place it was confined to geographically specific and limited areas. Quite often, moreover, the disputes were intra- rather than inter-communal. Indeed intra-communal clashes such as Shia-Sunni riots in the towns and cities of northern India were almost an annual occurrence.

Causes for the differences in the respective political structures of Pakistan (Indus) and India may not, therefore, be found entirely in the somewhat overstated communal divisions. By the same measure the communal divide, though significant, was not the sole reason for the partition of the subcontinent.

With the alighting of the East India Company upon its shores a more telling divide had begun to form in the subcontinent. Bengal, which was to become the real gateway to the Indian empire for the Company through the Ganges-Jumna waterway, laid the initial basis for this divide, which would manifest itself in the cleavage and contradiction between the feudal landowners on the one hand and the bourgeois merchants on the other. This landowner-bourgeois division, conceived initially in Bengal, was also to become the demarcating factor, in due course, between the Indus region (which became Pakistan) and the rest of India. Therein lay the seeds of Partition and, perhaps, the differing attitudes towards democracy. In Bengal of the late eighteenth century, however, this landowner-bourgeois divide was also, and alas, largely coterminous with the communal Muslim-Hindu divide.

By the close of the eighteenth century Bengal had already seen many defining events and processes: the initial and tentative trading operations of the Company in the seventeenth century which culminated in its emergence as a military power victorious on the field of Plassey (1757); the ensuing Plunder; the Famine; the Permanent Settlement and the destruction and uprooting of age-old relations of land tenure.

Foreclosure was not a concept with which Indian feudals had been familiar. They had always been in debt but had never lost their lands on that count. But the Company was a new element playing according to a fresh, and hitherto unknown set of rules. The Company was now enforcing new market laws. It was a commercial enterprise. Enforcement of contracts, rather than the maintenance of land tenure, was its main concern. As the Company expanded its commercial operations and clamped a vice-like military grip, the feudals, overwhelmingly Muslim, first went into debt and then lost their lands.

Land now came to be cultivated through rich rentiers profiting by the trading operations of the Company. The dispossessed landowners had mostly been Muslims. Most of the new rentiers were Hindu Marwaris. On the whole, the beneficiary of the Company's commerce, the trading class, was largely Hindu.

As the British set up trading posts in Bengal, Hindu traders, merchants and bookkeepers were, for half a century at least, the exclusive intermediaries of British trade in India. Even though they were relegated to subordinate posts by the 'Europeanization' policy pursued by Cornwallis, they remained the exclusive bureaucratic resource of the Company.

To the feudal (Hindu or Muslim), the position of an account keeper or munshi was anathema, even when he had lost his entire land-holding. The post was too inferior. Such jobs, in the age-old caste system, were for the vaish, a caste of Hindus historically entrusted with trade and bookkeeping. The response of the Bengali feudal to his fall from grace showed that however strongly Islam may have disclaimed the caste order as a Hindu practice, it had itself fallen victim to this all-pervading Indian scheme of things.

The feudal was suspicious of the new order. It had brought with it an altogether new value system, which was gradually shifting power to 'low caste' merchants. In the old order, land had been the symbol of wealth as well as of power. The two most honourable pursuits for the feudal lord were the right to collect land revenue, and the duty to raise a regiment in the service of the imperial authority, whosoever the king or emperor. Both these 'privileges' were linked to land and to the centuries-old dominion of the landlord over the peasant. Peasants were bound to surrender their surplus produce. They were also obliged to send their sturdiest youth to fight for the lord. But now the Company was introducing district collectors and salaried troops to replace the old system. The feudal landowners of Bengal, almost entirely Muslim, were out in the cold.

By contrast the community of Bengali merchants, almost entirely Hindu, profited by British trade. They took to it as other merchants in the past had done to Arab and East Indian coastal trade. Merchants had, in fact, always profited by trade. They were the beneficiaries of the significant overland trade with Central Asia and Iran through the northwestern passes. But there was a crucial difference between the past and the present, between the period of the Muslim invaders and the advent of the British. For the first time, the frontline Indian trader had the support and the productive resources of an industrial nation with more efficient means and modes of production, communication, transport and war than any previous invader or ruler had known.

This partnership between the Indian merchant and the British, forged early in the eighteenth century, was to last well into the nineteenth. In fact it lasted precisely upto the conquest by the British of the Indus region. This partnership helped the gradual growth of the bourgeoisie in the areas of India under the British. But for most of this time, until the mid-nineteenth century, Indus (which became Pakistan) was beyond British India. The Company's trade, creating with it a vibrant bourgeoisie, flourished in India, even though it mainly funnelled out enormous resources to Britain.

The conquest of Indus (Sindh in 1843 and Punjab, including the North West Frontier Province, in 1849) opened up new prospects for the colonial power. Vast tracts of potentially arable land were at its feet. As he began to map and chart these endless deserts and plains, the British officer envisioned a rich and prolific granary for the empire. He saw a new class of landlords as the key players in the Indus system.

The importance of this region was highlighted for another reason, too. In the Uprising of 1857, Indus had played a crucial role in support of the colonial power. It would henceforth become indispensable to the defence of the empire.

After the suppression of the Uprising of 1857, it was thus expedient for the British to switch partners. The merchant had paved the way, and paid for the armies to win the Empire. Now the landowner was needed to bring in the harvest. The British now began to strengthen, and to depend upon, the landowners. In the Indus region, in fact, they themselves first installed the feudals, then began to empower and use them.

This option was expedient. The plunder of the colonies had enabled Britain to graduate into an industrial empire. It had lubricated the Industrial Revolution. Now the colonial possessions were to be held as 'agrarian appendages' to the Lancashire cotton mills and the Dundee jute giants, as well as to feed the Royal armies and navies spread across the global empire. Thus the surplus produce of the native peasant had to be farmed out of the colony. The feudals were better at extracting produce and revenue from the peasant. This took the shape of crops: cotton, jute, wheat and sugar. The feudals helped in expropriating these from the peasant and surrendering them to the revenue officials and 'Collectors' of the imperial power.

This new arrangement was to the benefit of all parties to the compact. 'The feudal found himself propped up securely by the support of a strong and stable central authority, competent to punish "rebels and anarchists" in the remotest corners of the realm. The Raj discovered in the feudal order a workable machine for expropriating the peasant's surplus produce, while helping at the same time to maintain peace and order.'[3] The strong grip of the British administration also ended all internecine struggles for supremacy which, in the last one hundred and fifty years, had created fearsome deserts in central and northern India. 'For the next fifty years, the peasant had his peace, the feudal lord his prestige, while the imperial bureaucratic network was free to expropriate the produce of Indus and India.'[4] One hundred years after Plassey it was the turn of the Indian bourgeoisie to be left out in the cold.

There was one other, perhaps more significant, reason for the British to part company with the indigenous Indian mercantile and business classes: their increasing concern with potential competition. By this time, the Indian merchants and businesses were themselves becoming a force to be reckoned with. They had all along been investing their profits derived from imperial trade in small manufacturing units and related indigenous businesses. Imperial manufacturers had now begun to feel the fast growing competitive potential of Indian industry. In the half-century following 1857, a gradual squeeze was applied on Indian goods. 'All tariff duties were abolished in 1879 with a view to benefit Lancashire. In 1895, an excise duty of 5 per cent was imposed on Indian cotton goods with a view to countervailing a similar tariff on Lancashire goods imposed in the interests of revenue. The value of the Indian rupee in terms of the English pound was fixed in such a way as to help imports from England and discourage exports from India.'[5]

This 'switching of partners' was singularly propitious for the Indus region. The new partnership was dependent upon an unprecedented expansion in agriculture, because of huge irrigation projects. In comparison to India, the Indus had a weak mercantile or business class. The growth of the merchant and business classes was also impeded by the land revenue and land tenure systems introduced by the British, who now preferred to introduce a system of surplus-collecting 'landlords' called lambardars. These were grantees of land, as were all others 'settled' in 'colonized' areas. 'Colonization', as it was called, through allotment of lands, was undertaken after water was brought to previously parched and desert lands through an intricate matrix of barrages and canals. From 1880 onwards, peasant families were settled in various parts of the Indus region, as new lands were opened up in the newly constructed irrigation networks. The sizes of the holdings varied. Initially, the largest were between 100 and 150 acres, although a select few, who had served the British in the Uprising, were granted substantially larger tracts.

Then the Punjab Land Alienation Act was promulgated in 1900. This disqualified 'non-agricultural' tribes from acquiring the holdings of their 'agricultural' debtors. This was in sharp contrast to what had been the Company's policy in Bengal in the eighteenth century. In Bengal it had allowed non-landowning creditors to uproot the indebted landowner. Land had become a market commodity in Bengal, adding to the strength and resources of the bourgeoisie. The Punjab Land Alienation Act impeded this development.

The pre-emption laws, coupled with the Alienation Act, facilitated the landed gentry with larger holdings to acquire more and more adjoining pieces. Soon they became large landowners and absentee feudals. Land prices in the Punjab and other Indus areas began to rise steadily. Between 1866 and 1922 they rose from a mere Rs 10 to Rs 238 per acre. Political power followed economic power. An increase in the size and value of the landholdings led to an increase in the political influence of landowners and feudals. By the time of the First World War, therefore, these agro-feudal areas, specifically the Indus region, became steadfast bastions of the Raj. The Raj had begun by creating a communal Hindu-Muslim divide in Bengal. Its policies were now to create a major regional disparity between the Indus region and the rest of India.

This switching of allies was crucially significant to the future of the subcontinent. The bourgeoisie had helped the British win the empire. The feudals would now aid its consolidation. While the business classes were increasing their potential to compete with the imperial manufacturers, the feudals were to remain, by their inherent station, mere servile and complementary subordinates of the Empire. They had a commonality, rather than a contradiction, of interests with the British government. India had feudals (and princes) but also established and vibrant businesses and mercantile houses. Indus had only feudals and none of the latter. As Indus profited by the Raj, the trade and business classes of India began to compete with and resent imperial manufacturers.

By this time the Indian bourgeoisie had begun to reinvest its accumulated surpluses in its own private trades, businesses, and small industries. Initially, business families operated those industries and businesses that were not British monopolies by imperial decree. Later, through their skills and savings and their high sense of thrift, they began to compete with imperial manufactures even in sectors that were prohibitively taxed. The Indian textile sector, for example, had re-emerged, despite heavy excise duties designed to make it non-competitive.

As competition in economic interests began to intensify in the late nineteenth century, the Indian business classes also began to develop a nationalistic consciousness. They now sought to organize themselves economically and politically. These classes required both a trade organization to advance their substantial economic interests as well as a political party to win for them the necessary political privileges and economic space. 'It is, therefore, no mere coincidence that the Indian Chamber of Commerce and the Indian National Congress were established in the same year: 1885.'[6] This awakening of the business classes sought to rid all Indian domestic markets of foreign manufactures.

India had been defeated politically and militarily in the Uprising of 1857. But now an economic battle was about to be joined. There was, of necessity, some bourgeois simmering and unrest. There were calls to boycott imperial manufactures. New Hindu revivalist organizations and dynamic personalities came into the nationalist limelight. The Arya Samaj embraced all that was Indian, howsoever ancient. All that was foreign was denounced by Bal Gangadhar Tilak.

The British government reacted to this revivalism by promulgating a series of laws to suppress the bourgeois unrest. The first decade of the twentieth century witnessed the application of several strict laws. The Official Secrets Act of 1904 widened the scope of 'sedition' and restricted press criticism of the government. The Public Meetings Act, the Criminal Law (Amendment) Act, and the Seditious Meetings Act were adopted in 1907. 1908 brought the Explosive Substances Act and the Newspaper (Incitement to Offences) Act. The Indian Press Act was applied in 1910.

At this time, however, the mainstream Indian bourgeoisie was not in a position to confront either the British or the feudals. As an ever-expanding class of merchants and industrialists, it did of course aspire to replace the British and to take India as its own exclusive market. But this had to be done gradually. The militancy of Tilak and the Arya Samaj was likely to provoke communalism and cause schisms and fractures in the polity. That would reduce the market. A milder, gentler, and all-embracing policy had to be adopted. The philosophy and strategy of the Arya Samaj was thus overwhelmed by the pragmatism of the Congress of those early years. And the energetic and fiery Tilak lost the field first to the moderate Gopal Krishna Gokhale (1866-1915), and then to Mohandas Karamchand Gandhi.

Even as he lost ground, Tilak's pressure was significant. In the 1906 session, the Congress itself, through its president, none other than the mild Dadabhai Naoroji, demanded 'Swaraj' or self-rule. As the Congress demand shook the subcontinent, the colonial government reacted by arresting Tilak for sedition and by exiling him to Burma after a trial in Bombay. Jinnah, incidentally, played a significant role in these events. He acted as secretary to Naoroji and, upon Tilak's arrest, was one of his defence lawyers.

As these developments unfolded in India, Indus stayed calm, profiting by a larger agricultural produce than it had ever witnessed in history. The Indus landowner was becoming richer. Arable land had increased. There was enough water for all crops. The Punjab peasant was being inducted in the Imperial army. Unlike the Indian bourgeoisie, neither the Indus landowner nor the peasant had any conflict with the Raj. They were, indeed, integrated into it.

The First World War was significant in perpetuating the Indus-India divide. It impelled the British government to disperse industrial units to the subcontinent. In so far as it jeopardized all communications, transport, and all maritime trade routes in the world, it obliged the British to develop a second subsidiary industrial base for the empire. Britain was obliged to encourage indigenous Indian industry. The Parsee house of Jamshedji Tata had already set up a textile mill at Nagpur and a steel mill at Jamshedpur. Now the capacity of these mills was allowed to be enhanced. Tata also began to produce India's own locomotives, even though production and price were strictly controlled. As the British Indian Railways was the sole customer, Tata had his hands tied. All the industry was located in India, none in Indus. Indus remained an exporter of agricultural produce. But it also 'exported' another significant 'produce': the Punjabi and Pathan soldiers.[7] The War impelled the Imperial government to raise a vast army, which was (largely) raised in Indus. It thus expanded the Indian bourgeoisie, while further integrating Indus into the military system of the Raj.

While the British relaxed the restrictions on economic activities, they did not pursue the same liberal spirit in other fields. The First World War, therefore, brought in its wake more stringent restrictions on political activity, and the total loss of what little civil liberties there were. The Indus region saw one great tragedy in this period: the massacre at Jallianwala Bagh in Amritsar. It appeared that the Raj had lost its nerve, seeing such a large gathering in the Punjab. It had a telling effect on the thinking and resolve of some Punjabi youth who, in the decades that followed Jallianwala, took to more violent means to resist and overthrow the Raj, but it did not trigger off a mass resistance in the Indus region.

The impact in India was different. The greater and more draconian controls solidified the compact between the Indian bourgeoisie and the Indian National Congress. The Congress now became more vigorous in espousing the causes of the Indian craftsman and manufacturer. Like Tilak in the past, the Congress now began frequently to seek the boycott of foreign goods. Gandhi's spinning wheel became the national symbol of resistance to foreign manufactures.

As an aside, it may be mentioned that as in the 1857 Uprising, the princes of India, without distinction of religion, were foremost in support of the British war effort. The charge on Turkish Haifa was led by the Maharaja of Jodhpur's Lancers in September 1917. Most of the ranks were Muslims. Bikaner's Camel Corps was engaged at such distant places as China, Egypt, and Palestine. Gwalior contributed three battalions and a hospital ship. The list can go on but we must remain focused on the Indus-India divide.

The recruitment policy of the Raj during the War has been alluded to above. How enormous its effect was on the Indus-India disparity has yet to be elucidated. The War had opened up a major source of income to the Punjab and Indus peasant: recruitment in the subordinate ranks of the Indian Army. This process had actually begun in the preceding century. Michael O'Dwyer, who was the governor of Punjab at the time of the fateful Jallianwala Bagh massacre, had endorsed the praise and appreciation of the Punjabi soldier expressed by such authorities as Lords Roberts and Kitchener. He said that their argument 'was ... irrefutable that if India could only afford a small army of seventy-five thousand British (now reduced to under 60,000) and one hundred and sixty thousand Indian troops for the protection of a subcontinent of over 300 millions of people, it would be unwise to take any but the best Indian material and this was to be found mainly in the Punjab.'[8]

There was thus a significant Punjabization of the Indian Army preceding, during and after the War. Punjab began to be referred to as the 'sword arm of India'. In 1862, it had contributed as many as 28 out of the 131 units of infantry in the Indian Army. The proportion of Punjabi troops went up greatly by the turn of the century. When the First World War broke out in 1914 the number of Punjabi units in the Indian Army had risen to 57 out of 121, almost half from just one province. During the War it would rise even further. Indus had thus a larger and denser soldier-to-population ratio than anywhere else in India. During this period significant numbers of Pathans from the North West Frontier Province of the Indus region were also recruited. This concentrated praetorian environment had no parallel in any other region of the subcontinent.

The War took the Punjabi peasant-soldier to many parts of the world. He saw lands and technological advances that he had never envisioned. He was exposed to a new and different world beyond his cloistered village. His perspective was enlarged. He also felt the winds blowing in a new direction and the changing social order in the erstwhile Tsarist Russia. He was completely immersed in new thoughts and concepts when he returned to his bullock-cart, plough, and indebtedness after the War was over. His income was somewhat secured by a regular pension. He had many stories to tell. In a time-and-land-locked social capsule, this much-travelled 'cosmopolitan' rose to a new social status and acquired a new influence in society. Folk songs of the time reflected his growing social status and importance: *'Vasna fauji de naal, paanway boot sanay lat maaray'* (I will live with a soldier even if he kicks me with his boot on). Thus, even as the bourgeoisie moved up the social ladder in India, the soldier, having fought for alien masters, was gaining an aura and a mystique in the Indus region. The demarcation between democracy and praetorianism was gradually becoming vivid.

As we have noted, Indus was at the same time benefiting from the expanding irrigation networks, which were bringing previously desert and shrub lands under the plough. As Imran Ali has pointed out,[9] two institutions gained authority through 'agricultural colonization'. The first was the state bureaucracy exercising control over the process of land settlement and the operation of the canal network, including the most vital discretion to allocate and distribute water. This gave great leverage to bureaucrats over the landowner and the peasant. In the absence of any significant business and trading classes, this peculiar authority consolidated the bureaucracy in a pre-eminent position in all the vast areas of the NWFP, Punjab and Sindh, which thus came under the plough for the first time ever.

The other institution that gained power and status equal to that of the civil bureaucracy through this agricultural bonanza was the military. Its officers and personnel were the major recipients of the newly opened canal-irrigated lands. Vast areas were allocated to retiring soldiers and veterans of the World War. Since the Imperial army still depended on animal power for transport and traction, newly 'colonized' lands were also earmarked for grants for the breeding of military animals, particularly cavalry horses but also camels and mules. Since, as noted, the Indus region alone provided almost half the recruits to the Imperial army from the entire subcontinent, the overall proportion of land grants to military personnel in Indus was much larger than in the rest of India. This naturally 'consolidated the linkages between the military service, agricultural land and political power'.[10]

The transformation of Indus deserts and shrub lands into fertile and rich farmlands was not without purpose. These continued to provide raw produce to the textile giants of northern England. This area was to be the cotton-growing appendage to the textile mills of Lancashire. 'Firms such as Volkart Brothers and Ralli Brothers were extensively involved in commodity trade. The British Cotton Growing Association, based in Manchester, took large areas on lease for cotton production. These at one stage amounted to 70,000 acres, mostly in Lower Bari Doab Colony in the Punjab.'[11]

At the same time, the development of industries and the growth of industrial relations was consciously discouraged in these areas. Despite being a sugar and cotton producing area, Pakistan had only one sugar mill and one textile mill at the time of Partition in 1947.

Thus, what Imran Ali calls the 'British Imperialist antipathy towards fostering industrial capitalism' in the Indus area had another purpose as well. The colonial government wanted to co-opt the 'militarized upper peasant groups of Punjab'[12] who had previously eliminated the old Mughal elite and established their supremacy under the Sikhs. Recruitment might suffer if other means of livelihood were also available to them. Deprived of other opportunities by the time of the Second World War, the hardy Pathan and Punjab peasants were more than willing recruits in the Indian Army even when there was the peril of dying in action.

The Indus bourgeoisie therefore remained next to non-existent. What there was of it remained predominantly rural and agro-based. It was limited and tied to the economy of small 'mandi' towns and 'mufassil' cities. It mainly comprised advocates, journalists, teachers, petition writers, and small traders or 'arhties' in small towns and markets. It remained under the shadow and political influence of the feudal gentry and of the imperial bureaucracy. After all, the feudals were fully integrated into the imperial scheme of governance. They kept the King's peace and facilitated the expropriation of the peasant's surplus produce. They also contributed their scions to the lower and middle ranks of the officers' corps of the British Indian Army. And the imperial bureaucracy was itself the backbone of the entire system, the main frame that held it all together. It, alone, determined the space and status allowed to any section of society.

Political organizations in India and Pakistan had also developed at a different pace and in different directions. By 1947 the Indian National Congress had developed into a strong and countrywide political party with impressive organization and structures from the ground to the top. It achieved this status under the guidance of such tireless and dedicated leaders as Gandhi and Nehru. Democratic principles were infused in the Congress where a new president was regularly elected at the end of the prescribed tenure of the incumbent. Gandhi retained his influence, but not always a veto, despite the fact, or perhaps because of the fact, that he took no office in the Congress Party.

The Muslim League, on the other hand, established no

proper political structure in all its existence. It had skeletal organizations in some provinces but it opted to mobilize the masses on the basis of a vision and a slogan without spelling out any detailed or comprehensive programme or commitment. Incidentally, the only specific, and radical, manifesto it produced, the one for the 1946 elections in the Punjab, was itself proscribed by the Muslim League's own Punjab government after Partition.

The weaknesses of the Indus bourgeoisie, as compared to the Indian, have already been dwelt upon. But there was one other and most important element: namely a lack of a committed and courageous leadership of the quality available to the Indian bourgeoisie in the persons of Gandhi and the Nehrus. This it finally obtained in the 1940s in the person of the Karachi-born lawyer, Mohammad Ali Jinnah. But that final compact between the leader and the community took time to take effect.

As the Muslim League's message and slogan for an independent state for the Muslims began to find adherents amongst the broad Muslim masses, the League found itself in a Catch-22 situation. The Muslim masses and the Muslim bourgeoisie were responding enthusiastically to Jinnah's call. But both these classes were weak in Indus. And the feudals in that region were not prepared to join their ranks until a League victory became inevitable.

However, Jinnah reached out to the broad masses so effectively, despite the 1937 rout in the provincial elections, that the feudal gentry realized that its interest in the Indus region lay with the Muslim League. The landowners of Sindh took the lead with the feudal-dominated Sindh assembly adopting a resolution endorsing the Muslim League's pursuit of Pakistan. The Punjabi landowners were soon to follow. Sikandar Hayat, the Punjab premier and his landlord-dominated Punjab National Unionist Party embraced the League.

The feudal switch from Unionist to the League was finally sealed when Sir Khizr Hayat Tiwana succeeded Sikandar Hayat as Punjab premier. The younger Unionists, led by Mumtaz Daultana, Shaukat Hayat and Iftikhar Mamdot, revolted. Tiwana's ancestors had aided the British in the 1857 Uprising, as had Hayat's. He himself had campaigned vigorously to recruit soldiers from the Punjab for the British Indian Army which was locked in the life and death conflict of the Second World War. But while Tiwana might have been indispensable to the British, his appointment caused disappointment among rival groups of feudals. This provided the opportunity the Muslim League needed. The League cadres had enthused the broad masses into a vigorous campaign under the slogan 'Khizri Wazarat Torr Do' (Dissolve the Government of Khizr). Mumtaz Daultana, Shaukat Hayat and Iftikhar Mamdot joined the Muslim League. Khizr capitulated and made up with the League. Instantly the League slogan was revised. Crowds at once began to chant 'Taza Khabar Aie Hai, Khizr Hamara Bhai Hai' (News has just come in, Khizr is our brother).

Even though the League victory in the 1946 election was crucially the gift of feudal opportunism, there was one very positive aspect of the League movement and success. It routed Islamic fundamentalists in their aspiration to obtain the mandate of the Muslim masses of the subcontinent. The fundamentalists, by and large, held back from the Pakistan movement that was being led by the League. Their own widely publicized positions were that Islam, being a universal religion, and the entire Muslim peoples (Ummah) being one single indivisible political entity, no territorial state could be created in the name of Islam because neither any Muslim, nor indeed Islam, could be confined to physical and geographically defined borders. The fundamentalists asserted that such an attempt would be the very negation of the fundamental principles of Islam.

As we have seen, therefore, from the turn of the century to

Khizr's capitulation, the development of a vast canal-irrigated zone in the Indus basin had made it a surplus agrarian region where market towns had grown and expanded. Most of this business activity, however, had remained completely non-industrial during colonial rule. Several legislative measures, such as the Punjab Alienation of Lands Act of 1901 and the several laws piloted by Sir Chotu Ram in the 1930s, prevented expropriation of land by the non-agricultural castes and thus restricted the domain of mercantile and business capital. Traditional land-owning castes could not be displaced either in the open market or through mortgage foreclosures. This had retarded the transition even to agricultural capitalism.

In India between the World Wars, on the other hand, the bourgeoisie had developed to some maturity. It now overshadowed the princes and the feudal nobility in its leadership of the Indian peoples. In fact, the Indian National Congress was an almost entirely bourgeois movement, supported by the broad masses and the Indian peasantry. The Indian feudal remained isolated and removed from the nationalist struggle, apprehensive as much of British commerce as of its Indian counterpart. Little wonder that he became the first target of Congress reforms after Independence.

At the time of Partition, therefore, the socio-political system that Pakistan inherited from the Raj was distinct and different from the legacy obtained by India. Relatively speaking, but significantly, India had a strong and vibrant middle class led by rich and well established business houses. Pakistan had neither a bourgeoisie nor any rich business or industrial establishment. Despite the many vigorous and brave campaigns of the Bengal Lancers, and the Maratha and Sikh armies, the Raj left in India a tradition of civilian supremacy. Pakistan was a quasi-militarized society. India had seen a structured development of the Indian National Congress, which was able to contain, overwhelm and guide the energies of the imperial bureaucracy that India also inherited. By comparison, the weak structures of the Muslim League compelled it to abdicate and to concede disproportionate autonomy and space to the civil and military bureaucracy.

At Partition, therefore, India had an energetic middle class, a strong political structure with a countrywide organization of political cadres, and a subordinated civil and military bureaucracy. Pakistan had a strong feudal class, an insignificant bourgeoisie and an entrenched civil and military bureaucracy. Pakistan inherited a great deal of baggage from the Raj that was likely to impede its progress towards democracy and constitutionalism. Would it be able to subordinate these established, entrenched and vested interests to democratic aspirations?

PART II: POST-PARTITION PLAYERS AND TACTICS

The question often asked is: how did the civil and military bureaucracy wrest power from the politicians at the very outset of Pakistan's creation? The answer has to be that it never relinquished it. Jinnah was the only politician who could have subordinated the bureaucracy and the army to supreme democratic will. There are many instances of his having emphasized and reiterated the point that Pakistan was not to be a bureaucratic, autocratic or dictatorial state. He was particularly averse to military domination. In October 1947, he had himself been slighted when his army chief, the British General Douglas Gracey, disobeying his order, refused to send troops into Kashmir. Given the opportunity, Jinnah would surely have corrected this imbalance. He could never have tolerated a military intervention or even an overarching bureaucratic authority. But Jinnah died merely a year after Partition. There was now no other politician who could command the respect, admiration and obedience of the well-entrenched civil and military bureaucracy.

the civil and military bureaucracy

Under the Raj, the bureaucrats had enjoyed remarkable autonomy and independence. They had been free to report directly to the governors, disregarding the wishes, if any, of the Indian ministers. The process that thus ensued after 1947 was not one whereby the civil and military bureaucracy had to seize power. The process was one whereby it merely had to maintain and consolidate its pre-existing hold over the state. That autonomy and independence had now only to be formalized. To achieve this purpose, the bureaucracy had to formally and officially remove itself from the pale of administrative subordination and the oversight of political ministers. This process was in fact initiated by a clever bureaucrat during Jinnah's own lifetime.

Muhammad Ali, a senior official with long experience in the finance department, persuaded Jinnah to create the office of secretary general to the Government of Pakistan. Muhammad Ali was himself the first appointee to that office.

A cabinet resolution gave to the secretary general direct access to each secretary of every department and a supervisory authority over all the work that each was doing. Employing this authority, Muhammad Ali set up a 'Planning Committee of the Cabinet' of which secretaries of all ministries were members. The secretary general presided over the committee. In fact, therefore, the planning committee became the alternate, indeed the real 'cabinet'. Soon it usurped all the functions of the cabinet. The secretary general, presiding over the committee, became the virtual prime minister. Important matters were decided outside the meetings of cabinet and were taken directly to the prime minister or the governor general. When the cabinet did meet to discuss these same issues, it was merely to put its formal endorsement upon decisions that had already been taken. Thus bypassed by the bureaucracy and divested of decision-making powers, politicians began to look feeble and fickle. Often ministers were neither aware of the proposed agenda of cabinet meetings nor had been briefed by departmental officials regarding the pros and cons of any item on it. All civil servants were quick to discern that the centre of gravity was not the prime minister nor, after Jinnah's death, the governor general. They could see power being wielded 'by the secretary general on the advice of the secretaries.' The office of secretary general thus became the bastion of bureaucratic authority. In the three years that it existed it made a very effective contribution towards the consolidation of the bureaucratic grip on the political structure of Pakistan.

Ironically, even when the office of secretary general was finally abolished it was only to further consolidate the power of the bureaucracy. Another bureaucrat, Ghulam Mohammad, abolished the office of secretary general and the parallel cabinet for his own personal reasons. Upon assuming the office of governor general, the autocratic Ghulam Muhammad could brook no rival centre of authority and that too under another bureaucrat. So neither the purpose, nor the effect, of the abolition of this post was to decentralize control from the bureaucrats to the civilian politicians. It was only to shift it from one bureaucrat to another. The politician was still kept out of the loop. Ghulam Muhammad, in fact, was to further tighten the hold of the civil and military bureaucracy upon the state.

Alongside civil bureaucracy, the Pakistan Army also betrayed an urge to remain autonomous of political authority. The problem had begun early. The first two commanders-in-chief (C-in-C) were both British. Generals Sir Frank Messervey and Sir Douglas Gracey, besides reporting to the Government of Pakistan, also turned for guidance to their own superior, Field Marshall Sir Claude Auchinleck. This naturally created a duality of authority and control. Instances are quoted in which the commanders are said to have disregarded the defence ministry's, indeed even Jinnah's, instructions.

The first Pakistani C-in-C, General Ayub Khan, was appointed to that office in January 1951. A little over a year later, riots broke out in the Punjab against the minority sect of Ahmadis, followers of Mirza Ghulam Ahmad of Qadian. There was large-scale rioting and looting in Lahore. As is wont to happen when religious passions are aroused, the situation spun out of control of the civil administration. The military was handed complete control of the city and its environs. It imposed martial law, Pakistan's first in any area. It immediately restored law and order. This would be normal in any democracy: a military commander obeying civilian orders. But the local military commander used the cover of martial law to do much more. He clamped down on the markets, freezing prices and ensuring hygiene. He arrested known smugglers and hoarders of essential commodities. The army thereby enhanced its position in the polity. This increment in its status enabled General Ayub Khan to wangle, from the weak and divided civilian administration, a four-year extension in the tenure of his service. Governor General Ghulam Muhammad obliged Ayub to win his loyalty. But it was also a significant incremental step for the general himself. It enhanced his personal stature, authority and influence in the state structures, though not necessarily his respect in political circles.

As Muhammad Ali and Ghulam Muhammad served to consolidate bureaucratic control, and as General Ayub Khan assiduously awaited the opportunity to take over the governance of the state, politicians were in a political tailspin. Jinnah's death in September 1948 had left a gaping void that none was large enough to fill. A diminutive Khwaja Nazimuddin was elevated to the office of governor general. Then, in October 1951, Prime Minister Liaqat Ali Khan was assassinated in Rawalpindi. Khwaja Nazimuddin now moved to the office of prime minister and the hard-as-nails bureaucrat, Ghulam Mohammad, became the governor general. Nazimuddin was from East Pakistan. He was a weak man and a series of events were to destabilize his government without great difficulty.

We have noticed how the anti-Ahmadi riots strengthened the political position of the army. But the riots also divided and weakened the civilian polity. They brought the fundamentalists into prominence. Jinnah had, in 1946, inflicted a crushing blow upon the Islamic fundamentalist parties. They had overwhelmingly opposed the concept of Pakistan. In the six years from 1947 to 1953, the fundamentalists had been clueless, rudderless and out at sea. Suddenly the anti-Ahmadi movement sparked life into the dying embers of religious fanaticism in Pakistan.

In 1953, many fundamentalist religious elements who had opposed the formation of Pakistan joined hands in a movement against the Ahmadis. We have seen how the army was inducted into the effort to put down the movement. The army had gained thereby. But so did the agitating fundamentalists. As the army gained in respect, and the fundamentalists gained confidence, democracy suffered.

The failure of the civil administration to enforce order and to bring religious zealotry under control, undermined the civilian government. Prime Minister Nazimuddin's writ was eroding fast. He was seen as weak and indecisive. Now rumours spread of an impending food shortage in the country. Reports were exaggerated to indicate prospects of a widespread famine. Austerity measures had to be adopted. A reduction in the defence budget by one-third was also proposed. This was not popular with the army. At an emergency food conference called in Karachi, the C-in-C and senior bureaucrats humiliated the prime minister, accusing him of weakness and indecisiveness. Nazimuddin's writ was no more. In April 1953, he was dismissed by the governor general. Pakistan's ambassador to the United States, Muhammad Ali Bogra, was nominated prime minister. Such was the bureaucrat's supremacy in the political field that Bogra immediately won a vote of confidence in the legislative assembly.

Agitational tempers had hardly cooled down in the Punjab, and political uncertainty still gripped the capital Karachi, when a new challenge arose. Early in 1954, provincial elections were held in East Pakistan and the United Front (a coalition of three political parties opposed to the Muslim League, viz., the Awami Muslim League, the Krishak Sramik Party and the Nizam-e-Islam Party) inflicted a crushing blow upon the ruling Muslim League. But the rulers in Karachi derided it as the 'Jugtu Front'. So the United Front provincial government in East Pakistan was not allowed to function. It was dismissed on charges of incompetence soon after it was formed. Troops were moved out to put down any resistance in East Pakistan.

Although Governor General Ghulam Muhammad had thus subverted the United Front government, its victory had emboldened members of the central assembly. They sensed the popular mood. They realized that the bureaucratic rulers were not in step with the people. They saw an opportunity to reduce the powers of the governor general. The assembly accordingly adopted an amendment in the Government of India Act 1935 providing that ministers would be individually and collectively responsible to the federal legislature and no longer hold the office subject to the pleasure of the governor general.

Governor General Ghulam Muhammad was not one to take such a move lying down. He reacted by declaring a state of Emergency and dissolving the assembly itself. At the same time, he appointed a new cabinet retaining Bogra as prime minister but inducting, most significantly, General Ayub Khan, the C-in-C, as the defence minister. Although Ayub occupied that post for just a year, this was a most portentous development. It has had an indelible, seemingly irreversible, effect on the history of Pakistan. Henceforth, the C-in-C would be his own boss. Henceforth, Ayub would personally steer the Pakistan Army to an entrenched position on the commanding heights of Pakistan's political landscape. I will examine, in due course, the long-term and deep-seated impact of this event.

The dissolution of the assembly was unsuccessfully challenged in the courts by the president of the Constituent Assembly, Maulvi Tamizuddin Khan.[13] However, in a subsequent follow-up judgment (1955)[14] Pakistan's Federal Court ruled that the governor general could not govern the country without a legislative assembly and that he was bound to 'bring into existence a representative legislative institution'. Having said so, the court proceeded to give the governor general an amazing power: to nominate the electorate.

The governor general was obviously relieved. The elite feared general elections. That was avoided. A democratic process, howsoever shamefacedly sham, was a necessary veneer. That was provided. The governor general thereupon decreed that a new Constituent Assembly would be elected, not by the general electorate but solely by the members of the provincial legislatures and that too by a method of proportional representation with a single transferable vote. This ensured, of course, that no party would have a majority in the new, indirectly elected, assembly and that the governor general would continue to call all the shots.

The fascination of the civil and military establishment with indirect or controlled elections and with manageable, restricted electorates was not surprising. The elite was in no doubt that an electoral process would not be favourable to it or its interests. This was the primary reason why the elite did not strive to give the country a constitution. A constitution would have automatically entailed the need for a fresh mandate through free and fair general elections. The elite obviously preferred some means that would have the 'form of elections' without the jeopardy of losing them. I will show that this obsession with 'controlled democracy' is a constant and autocratic thread that runs through the entire electoral history of Pakistan. However, to revert to 1955.

Bogra had been retained as prime minister upon dissolution of the assembly and even upon the re-constitution of the new assembly under guidelines provided by the Federal Court. But Bogra could not maintain the support of a majority for long. He was shown the door in 1955.

The same year, after some compromises and inevitable horse-trading, a coalition of the Muslim League and the United Front elected the former finance minister (and erstwhile secretary general) Mohammad Ali as prime minister. As noted, Muhammad Ali was a hard working, clever and scheming bureaucrat. He took up the task of constitution-making in earnest.

One major conundrum had bedevilled the West Pakistan elite. The Urdu- and Punjabi-speaking elite of West Pakistan had always feared East Pakistan's majority, a natural corollary to its larger population. It apprehended that the smaller units of West Pakistan (such as Sindh, Baluchistan, NWFP and Bahawalpur) would gang up with East Pakistan to overwhelm the Punjab and Karachi. The rulers at the Centre endeavoured to ward off the radical politics of East Pakistan. Therefore by an administrative order all the four provinces and the several autonomous states of West Pakistan were merged into one administrative and political entity: the 'One Unit'.

With the merger of all the West Pakistan units into one, a federation of two units only was created. And thereafter 'parity of representation' between East Pakistan and West Pakistan was adopted as the federal basis of Pakistan's first Constitution adopted in 1956. Administratively the One Unit was an easy trick. Politically it was a disaster. But Muhammad Ali was thereby able to cleverly pilot the constitution-making process. Not being a politician, however, he could not retain the loyalty of his colleagues for long. He was forced to resign in September 1956. A procession of three prime ministers, Hussain Shaheed Suhrawardy, I.I. Chundrigar and Firoz Khan Noon, followed. Ian Talbot has put it graphically: 'Prime Ministers moved through the revolving doors of office with increasing rapidity as power slipped from Karachi to the army headquarters in Rawalpindi.'[15] It is thus a trite observation that while India in its first decade had one prime minister and several army chiefs, Pakistan had several prime ministers and one army chief. Stability in the one office and instability in the other institution naturally reflected upon their power denominations *inter se*.

As prime ministers came and went, General Ayub Khan and the bureaucrats continued to consolidate their positions. The general had, indeed, always been pondering political issues. In later years, he himself claimed to have been the very initiator, in 1954, of the 'One Unit' concept. His influence remained substantial. And he felt himself free to trespass on the civilian domain, a tradition thereafter adopted by all his successors. On one occasion he wrote to the defence minister seeking the dismissal of the navy chief as 'he neither has the brain, imagination or depth of thought to understand such problems, nor the vision and ability to make any contribution'.[16] On another occasion, he sent off a stiff note to the prime minister seeking the dismissal of the governor of the State Bank of Pakistan for 'talking through his hat'.[17]

The tragedy is that no politician or civilian superior challenged, chastized or resisted Ayub. None even tried to read him the law or the rules of government business to remind him of his due station in life. None cautioned him. None reprimanded him. None issued him a notice to show cause. None chose to remove him.

Continuing musical chairs among the politicians did not threaten Ayub or the civil and military bureaucrats. They were alarmed only when it was announced that a free and fair general election with adult suffrage would be held in February 1959. The clock now began to tick for the elitist clique. Even the distant prospect of that eventuality was too much for the civil and military bureaucracy. A genuinely elected and refreshed assembly would most likely have the will, the mandate and the authority to tame the wild cats and to strip them of their powers.

How irked Ayub was at the thought of elections is evident from the entry in his diary which reads: 'The elections, of course, are coming near. The politicians have worked themselves into a state of hydrophobia (sic), especially the dismissed ones. They are dying to get back into power by hook or by crook. And having got there, they know they will have nothing to show for themselves except further disrupting the country. In which case they will come face to face with me and the army. Hence, I am regarded by them as Enemy Number 1 for doing my duty and trying to save the country. Their conscience is so deadened that in order to obtain a monetary gain, they will not even stop at destroying this army, the only shield they have.'[18]

By this time Ayub had, however, another worry on his mind. And this was personal. He had been appointed C-in-C in January 1951 for a term of four years. Before January 1955, Governor General Ghulam Mohammad had extended Ayub's tenure for another four years. That step had militated against military traditions but had suited both the governor general and the army commander. Now approaching January 1959, his benefactor was dead but Ayub was himself the major player on the scene. He expected a four-year extension by divine right. Another Ayub, (Ayub Khuhro), was the defence minister. According to Khuhro's biographer, (his daughter, Hamida), the general actually applied for a four-year extension, but was given only two by the civilian government. He felt slighted.[19]

With weak and unpopular 'revolving-door' administration at the centre, the economy flagged. Rising prices caused labour unrest and widespread disaffection. Then, in late September 1958, the deputy speaker of the East Pakistan assembly died after receiving injuries in a fracas on the floor of that house. Ian Talbot describes the situation succinctly: 'The Byzantine goings-on in Karachi were positively gentlemanly compared to the bear-pit in Dhaka where the physical violence during a debate on 21 September 1958 resulted in the death of Deputy Speaker Shahid.'[20] On 6 October, the Khan of Kalat, the most prominent princely ruler of Baluchistan, announced secession. On 8 October, President Iskandar Mirza, who had succeeded Ghulam Muhammad, imposed martial law. General Ayub Khan was nominated as the chief martial law administrator. On 27 October the general ousted the president. He thereupon also assumed unto himself the office of president of Pakistan.

General Ayub gave a new Constitution (of 1962) and introduced many reforms. But the most significant and profound consequence of the military takeover was that soon, though almost imperceptibly, Pakistan was converted from a state concerned primarily with the welfare of its citizens to one preoccupied with national security. This conversion from a welfare state to a national security state was, of course, a necessary and logical corollary of the turn of events. Unlike a minor temporary intervention in aid of the civil power, long-term and comprehensive military rule can only be justified by a perceived need to address some perennial threat to the security of the state. Without such a perception, army rule could not be defended.

The 1948 Indo-Pak conflict and subsequent tensions over water resources, the division of assets and over trade after India devalued its rupee but Pakistan did not, had caused considerable bitterness between the two neighbours. Yet India was not perceived as a real threat to Pakistan's security. Pakistan saw India as an illegal occupant of the state of Jammu and Kashmir but not as a threat to Pakistan's existence. Relations between the two states remained far better than they are now described as having been. Visas were easy to come by. Indian films were box office hits in Pakistan. Madhubala, Nargis, Dilip Kumar and Raj Kapoor adorned massive billboards and were household icons several decades before sitting-room video viewing reintroduced them. Sports competitions were frequent. Cross-border matches in cricket, volleyball, hockey, kabaddi, football drew substantial crowds. General Ayub himself inked in 1960 the Indus Waters Treaty that divided between India and

Pakistan the waters of the five Punjab rivers that drained into the Indus.

In the 1950s General Ayub, as C-in-C (and even as defence minister for one year) had guided Pakistan into treaty arrangements with the US and obtained substantial military hardware, profiting thereby from America's communist-phobia. Ayub's own view as army chief was clear: 'I was certain of one thing,' he was later to recall, 'Pakistan's survival was vitally linked with the establishment of a well-trained, well-equipped and well-led army.'[21] But to justify its continued all-embracing rule for a prolonged and indefinite period, the army had to find a new, more dramatic, rationale for it. Regretting that it had not taken advantage of the 'strategic opportunity' provided by the 1962 Sino-Indian conflict, it challenged India in the Rann of Kuch in 1964 and provoked a full-scale war over Kashmir in 1965. From a less than friendly neighbour, India was converted into a hostile enemy. India's hostility towards Pakistan was now shown as providing a complete justification for the otherwise illegitimate military rule.

There were other ways in which General Ayub Khan consolidated the army's position in the affairs and running of the state. His own personal experience was to shape the subsequent course of events in significant ways. Until he was made defence minister in October 1954 he had, as C-in-C, been reporting to the defence minister. He had taken all his orders from above, even though he may have often influenced the nature of those orders. But as defence minister, the C-in-C began reporting to himself. The prime minister was often engaged in political wranglings. With the office of army chief and defence minister merged into one, and outside the political fray, the military establishment attained enormous, and unprecedented autonomy from its political masters. A tradition was established that the army chief would virtually be his own boss. Appointments, transfers, and promotions in the military became the sole prerogative of the army chief. Thereafter, serving brigadiers and generals, subordinate to the chief, were inducted into key positions in the defence ministry. The tradition continues and enables the army chief to influence, even to determine, the policies of the defence ministry. Couple this with the parliamentary tradition of passing the entire defence budget, as framed by the military, without a debate, or even a vote, and you have a military 'state within a state'. The army's hold on the political system and its autonomy from political bosses and from parliamentary oversight, even in periods of civilian democratic rule, has thus been assured.

When, after a full decade in power, Ayub's grip began to loosen in the wake of a widespread popular uprising, the military commanders thought it was their birthright to succeed him. They, alone, could guide Pakistan towards civilized democracy. When resigning, in March 1969, Ayub ought to have handed over the office of president to the speaker of the National Assembly in accordance with the Constitution (of 1962) which he had himself promulgated. Instead, he invited General Yahya Khan, the then commander-in-chief, to take over the reins of power. Martial law was again proclaimed to facilitate Yahya's takeover and Ayub's own Constitution was abrogated by his successor in March 1969.

General Yahya held Pakistan's first free and fair general elections in December 1970 but he and his generals were reluctant to part with power. There was a popular uprising in East Pakistan, which the generals again tried to crush by military means. The civil war ended with the intervention of the Indian Army and the defeat and surrender of Pakistan's Eastern Command on 16 December 1971. East Pakistan thus became Bangladesh.

In (West) Pakistan, the defeated military commanders, no longer able to hold on to power, invited Zulfiqar Ali Bhutto, the majority leader in that part of the broken country, to form a government. Bhutto can be credited with piloting, by unanimous vote, Pakistan's third Constitution through the

National Assembly in 1973. But even though this Constitution specifically and expressly subordinated the military to democratic will, and although the military had been humiliated – 90,000 troops and others had been taken prisoner, and the morale of the soldier and the officer was low – Bhutto chose not to take any advantage of that opportunity to reduce praetorianism, even while introducing wide-ranging reforms in every other sector of society. The scope, success or failure of those reforms are not within the ambit of this limited study. Their effect was indeed multi-faceted and would need critical and unbiased examination. Here my focus remains on praetorianism and its shadow on democratic structures.

In fact, Bhutto himself somewhat lengthened that shadow. He at once took on the task of rehabilitating the competence and morale of the Pakistan Army. By deftly negotiating the 1972 Simla Pact, Bhutto brought back all Pakistani prisoners. He ordered that they be garlanded by officials and partymen at entry points on the border in the full gaze of television cameras and press photographers. He then sought to upgrade the military's defence capability, especially by inducting the nuclear option. But would Bhutto be rewarded for this? Bhutto's own ultimate fate, his ouster and arrest by his own appointed army chief, his execution on a trumped-up charge and the verdict of the superior judiciary on oath of allegiance to the will and laws of his military detractor, highlight another compact that, having been formalized early, had by now solidified: the compact between the civil and military establishment and the superior judiciary. Together they have smothered democratic structures and processes, even though politicians cannot be absolved of their own share of the blame.

the superior judiciary

The judiciary has, throughout Pakistan's existence, been consistent and constant in one respect. It has always legitimized authoritarian and military interventions in the political structures of Pakistan. Not once has it invalidated the incumbent regime of a military adventurer.

Since the ruling elite was, as submitted above, averse to holding general elections and, in fact, held none for the first twenty-three years, it sought legitimacy by other means. Unhappily the judiciary always seemed all too willing to provide it. Hamza Alavi has pointed out that 'the thread that runs centrally through the history of Pakistan is a tension between the locus of power and legitimation of power.'[22] The superior judiciary has consistently helped the locus to 'legitimate' its power.

We have seen that the first instance when the superior judiciary lent itself to an executive head as a legitimizing force was in 1955. We have seen how Governor General Ghulam Mohammad dissolved the Constituent Assembly in October 1954. The president of the assembly, Maulvi Tamizuddin Khan, challenged the dissolution before the Sindh Chief Court. The Sindh Court restored the dissolved assembly. The federal government appealed. According to Hamida Khuhro, the governor general had summoned Chief Justice Mohammad Munir ahead of the dissolution and warned him not to restore the assembly. The chief justice obliged.[23] By a majority of four to one, the Federal Court accepted the appeal on a technical ground and thereby dismissed Maulvi Tamizuddin's challenge to the dissolution.[24]

The technicality on which the challenge to the dissolution had been dismissed affected several enactments. The Federal Court ruled that the Sindh chief court had had no jurisdiction to resurrect the assembly because the amendment which it purported to invoke to do so was unconstitutional and hence void. The Sindh court could not have issued any writ under the law as the empowering bill had not been presented to the governor general for assent. As such the bill had no legal effect and could not vest in the Sindh court the authority to review executive action. Even though the Federal Court did not rule the dissolution valid that was enough to put paid to the Sindh court and the assembly. However, this decision raised further questions. Several other laws had also not been presented to the governor general in the mistaken belief that his assent was not required because, as a representative of the British Crown, he was no longer the sovereign after Pakistan had obtained its freedom. Thus, as a result of the Federal Court's verdict, as many as forty-six acts were nullified.

Now an anomalous situation arose. The assembly had been dissolved. There was no legislature. There was a legal vacuum. And several laws were no more. How could these laws be applied? Who would approve and validate the budget? There was constitutional paralysis.

In an attempt to resolve the impasse, the governor general himself promulgated what was described as the Emergency Powers Ordinance of 1955 (EPO). Through this measure he purported to assume the powers to frame a constitution, to validate laws and to devise and approve the country's budget.

One Usif Patel was arrested under a detention law that the governor general had endeavoured to validate through the EPO. He challenged the law. Smitten by the adverse criticism of his judgment in the Tamizuddin case, the chief justice tried to regain lost prestige. He declared the ordinance *ultra vires,* that is, in conflict with the Constitution and hence illegal. He ruled that 'the Governor General can give or withhold his assent to the legislation of the Constituent Assembly but he himself is not the Constituent Assembly and on its disappearance he can neither claim powers which he never possessed nor claim to succeed to the powers of that Assembly.'[25] The governor general had cut short the legislative assembly. And now the court had cut off his hands.

This was possibly Chief Justice Munir's finest hour. But it was a flash in the pan. He would soon adopt an insidious doctrine that would sanction a chain of constitutional subversions by military commanders in the future history of Pakistan.

In the constitutional vacuum thus created by Usif Patel the federal government again turned to the court for rescue. The court had itself effectively condoned the dissolution of the assembly. Then it had denied the governor general any legislative authority. What was to be done?

The obvious answer would have been a fresh general election. But the elite wanted to 'legitimate' the processes and structures of governance without any exposure to the verdict of the people. They turned again to the Federal Court and the court bailed them out in its Opinion on the Governor General's Reference of 1955.[26]

The court decreed that an elected and representative Constituent Assembly was a sine qua non. It thus directed the governor general to immediately arrange for elections to a fresh assembly but curiously, as we have seen in another context, allowed him to determine the electorate. It also used this belated opportunity to expressly validate the dissolution, something it had not done, to the ire of the governor general, in the Tamizuddin judgment. To validate the dissolution, however, the court leaned upon the doctrine of necessity as *'salus populi suprema lex'*[27]. This doctrine, thus injected into the chequered constitutional history of Pakistan, continues to subvert democratic structures and to provide unceasing justification to praetorian interventions. Its most famous application was in 1958.

We have seen how a Constitution had been adopted in 1956 by the new Constituent Assembly and how it was abrogated upon the promulgation of martial law in October 1958. Munir was still the Chief Justice of Pakistan. On 13 and 14 October, he presided over a bench hearing appeals in certain criminal matters pending since 1957. If the military takeover was valid, the courts' jurisdiction to hear these appeals had abated by the express intent of a presidential order promulgated on 10

October 1958. Not otherwise. Munir took no time to validate the military takeover. In State versus Dosso (1958)[28] he declared that:

> If the attempt to break the Constitution fails, those who sponsor or organize it are judged by the existing Constitution as guilty of the crime of treason. But if the revolution is victorious in the sense that the persons assuming power under the change can successfully require the inhabitants of the country to conform to the new regime, then the revolution itself becomes a law-creating fact because thereafter its own legality is judged not by reference to the annulled Constitution but by reference to its own success... Thus a victorious revolution or a successful coup d'etat is an internationally recognized legal method of changing a Constitution.

Could a wider door have been left open for any future military adventurer? There certainly would be more to come. And, equally certainly, the court would have more such matters to resolve in subsequent decades.

Technically the Dosso judgment (1958) was overruled by the Supreme Court itself in 1972 but that later judgment was only an *ex post facto* condemnation of a military usurper after his fall. The backdrop to that pronouncement has also been briefly alluded to above in another context.

When General Yahya Khan fell from grace and power on the surrender of the Pakistan Army in Dhaka in December 1971, Zulfiqar Ali Bhutto, who commanded the support of the majority of the elected parliamentarians from West Pakistan, was invited by the military commanders to take over. Bhutto took over as president and chief martial law administrator. One of his early orders was decreeing the arrest of Malik Ghulam Jilani, a leading Punjabi politician. Jilani was arrested under a martial law regulation originally promulgated by Yahya Khan. Jilani's daughter, Asma, filed a habeas corpus petition. Soon the Supreme Court was again engaged in discussing the validity of military interventions.

Bhutto was obviously interested in obtaining a verdict that would condemn military adventurers and close the door that the Dosso judgment (1958) had left wide open. General Yahya, whose military regime and laws were the subject of judicial scrutiny, was already disgraced and in custody. The military, having been humiliated in East Pakistan, could hardly overawe anyone at that time. Chief Justice Hamoodur Rehman was himself from East Pakistan and had now decided to settle permanently in (West) Pakistan. This time the court was eloquent in its condemnation of military interventions.[29] The court declared that Dosso (1958) was bad law. In the words of the chief justice:

> I am not aware of any document or of any provision in any law which gives the Commander of the armed forces the right to proclaim Martial Law, although I am prepared to concede that he has, like all other loyal citizens of the country, a bounden duty to assist the State, when called upon to do so ... This country was not a foreign country which had been invaded by any foreign army with General Agha Muhammad Yahya Khan at its head nor was it an alien territory which had been occupied by the said army. The question of imposition of "military rule" as an incident of *jus belli* of international law could not, in the circumstances, possibly have arisen ... Looked at, therefore, either from the constitutional point of view or the Martial Law point of view, whatever was done in March 1969, either by Field Marshal Muhammad Ayub Khan or General Agha Muhammad Yahya Khan, was entirely without any legal foundation.

In no uncertain terms the chief justice declared the Dosso judgment as being unconstitutional. He observed that:

> The principle enunciated by him (former Chief Justice Munir) is, in my humble opinion, wholly unsustainable, and I am duty bound to say that it cannot be treated as good law either on the principle of *stare decisis* or even otherwise.

Justice Yaqub Ali was more poetic in his condemnation of all military adventurers. Wistfully he declared that:

> My own view is that a person who destroys the national legal order in an illegitimate manner cannot be regarded as a valid source of law-making. May be, that on account of his holding the coercive apparatus of the State, the people and the Courts are silenced temporarily, but let it be laid down firmly that the order which the usurper imposes will remain illegal and Courts will not recognize its rule and act upon them as *de jure*. As soon as the first opportunity arises, when the coercive apparatus falls from the hands of the usurper, he should be tried for high treason and suitably punished. This alone will serve as a deterrent to would be adventurers.

Yahya was of course a military general, even when he was in custody. The army could not countenance his trial. He could not be tried, as even under the dynamic Bhutto civilian democratic institutions were powerless against the military leviathan.

Despite the pious wish articulated by Justice Yaqub Ali, Yahya was thus never tried. But the court would nevertheless itself soon be put on trial. All the pious and self-righteous exclamations of the Jilani case in 1972 were dropped like hot bricks when, despite these definitive prohibitions, General Zia-ul-Haq deposed Prime Minister Zulfiqar Ali Bhutto and imposed martial law in July 1977.

On the night of 5 July, Bhutto was arrested. His wife Begum Nusrat sought relief from the Supreme Court pleading that in the light of the Jilani case no military commander could impose martial law. The military government being without lawful authority, she submitted, the arrest of her husband decreed by the military commander was illegal. In its judgment in the Begum Nusrat Bhutto case (1977) the court hastily, but unabashedly, resiled from its judgment in the Jilani case (1972).

The judgment in Begum Nusrat Bhutto's case (1977) was founded formally and squarely on the expeditious doctrine of necessity. It was settled by a court presided over by Chief Justice Anwarul Haq who had personally benefited from an amendment in the Constitution made by General Zia as chief martial law administrator. And it echoed the principal basis of Munir's judgments in his Opinion on the Governor General's Reference (1955) and the Dosso case (1958).

Bhutto's petition had first come up for hearing on 20 December 1977 before a bench presided over by Chief Justice Yaqub Ali. Yaqub had, in the Jilani case, declared that the usurper would be put on trial. The court had issued a notice to the government and entertained the petition for a full hearing. It had also directed that Bhutto be brought to Rawalpindi for the hearing. The military rulers became apprehensive. On 22 September, the Constitution was amended by a military decree to oust Yaqub Ali and to appoint Anwarul Haq as chief justice of Pakistan. The case was thus heard by a court presided over by a chief who was a direct beneficiary of Zia's purported power to amend the Constitution. If Zia were declared illegal, the chief justice would also, ipso facto, cease to be chief justice. The court heard the case through October and pronounced judgment on 10 November 1977.[30]

In the leading judgment subscribed by the chief justice himself, the court concluded that Zia's takeover was an 'extra-constitutional step' but was justified on grounds of state necessity and the welfare of the people. It added that 'this is not a case where the old Legal Order has been completely suppressed or destroyed, but merely a case of constitutional deviation for a temporary period and for a specified and limited objective, namely the restoration of law and order and normalcy in the country and the earliest possible holding of free and fair elections for the purposes of the restoration of democratic institutions under the 1973 Constitution.'

It is another matter that the courts continued to condone and provide unquestioned recognition to Zia's military regime for an unspecified and indefinite period. Zia was to benefit by this judgment for eleven years until his death, still as president and army chief, in a plane crash in August 1988.

In this judgment, however, the chief justice was required to take another leap of faith. That is a measure of the subordination of the judiciary to the military will and hence, too, a measure of the impediments in the way of democracy and sovereign democratic institutions in Pakistan. On the promulgation of martial law, all Supreme Court judges had been required to swear an oath to the military government. This fresh oath was at variance, indeed in conflict, with the oath they had earlier taken to 'protect, uphold and defend the Constitution' (of 1973). The new oath, dictated by Zia, omitted these crucial words. How could the judges, bound thus to the Constitution, take another oath in violation of the self-same Constitution they had sworn to 'protect, uphold and defend' and even before they had ruled on the validity of the new regime? But Chief Justice Haq had no problem overcoming any difficulty. He expressed the view that the new oath did not 'in any manner restrict the independence of the superior judiciary nor affect their obligation to perform their judicial functions according to law; it only indicates that the superior judiciary, like the rest of the country, has accepted the fact, which is even otherwise also evident, that on the 5th of July 1977, a radical transformation took place in the pre-existing Legal Order.' Another judge, Qaisar Khan, was far more forthright, candid and blunt. 'However,' he observed, 'under the President's Post Proclamation Order 9 of 1977, we were directed to take a new oath or to quit. As a result of the said directive we took the new oath.'

The pious hopes that the Jilani judgment (1972) had raised, even though that too had been an *ex post facto* decision, were now dashed by the Nusrat Bhutto judgment. And twelve years later, the judiciary would build a mausoleum over this grave of the Jilani judgment after the military takeover by General Pervez Musharraf in October 1999.

Between generals Zia and Musharraf the Supreme Court displayed some judicial activism. When Zia dissolved his own assembly in May 1988, the Supreme Court held the dissolution invalid, although it refused to restore the assembly. It was reported that before the judgment could be announced, the new army chief, who had taken over on Zia's death, had sent a message to the court through Zia's law minister that restoration of the assembly would not please the military establishment.[31] The court was said to have already finalized its judgment but was persuaded by the message to change the last paragraphs denying relief to the petitioner and refusing to restore the assembly on the ground that a fresh election had already been scheduled.

During the ensuing successive administrations of Benazir Bhutto and Nawaz Sharif, the court displayed more sparks of judicial activism. When Nawaz Sharif's government was dismissed and the assembly dissolved by decree of a civilian president in April 1993, the court restored the government and the assembly. When Prime Minister Benazir Bhutto wanted to appoint some judges to the superior courts, the court dismissed most of her appointees and asserted a right to determine judicial appointments. When ruling party workers stormed the Supreme Court in November 1997, the court summoned Prime Minister Nawaz Sharif in person to appear before it on a charge of contempt of court. When parliament legislated anti-terrorist laws, the court struck them down. When the Sharif government introduced military courts in the wake of an insurgency and the breakdown of law and order, the court declared them illegal. All these judgments were rendered when civilian democratic administrations were in place.

Then in October 1999, Army Chief General Pervez Musharraf suspended the Constitution, arrested the prime minister and imposed military rule over the country. The Supreme Court was once again called upon to determine the validity of the military takeover.

Zafar Ali Shah had been a member of the dissolved National Assembly. A bench of twelve judges of the Supreme Court headed by Chief Justice Irshad Hassan Khan heard Shah's petition challenging the military takeover. Once again, the judges had been compelled to take an oath prescribed by the military commander which was at variance with the oath each one of them had taken under the Constitution of 1973. Chief Justice Khan had taken the oath after the incumbent refused to take it. This time, however, the court, in its departure from the oath its members had already taken, was facilitated by the ousted prime minister Nawaz Sharif's own lawyer and former law minister when he himself submitted that, 'a judge in his conscience and in good faith may decide to resign or he may decide in the higher public interest he would retain office as has been done by the judges of this court and other judges of the Superior Judiciary.'[32] But despite having taken an oath from which again the words 'to protect, uphold and defend the Constitution' had significantly been omitted, the chief justice was at pains to justify its administration upon the judges. Drawing from such diverse and unlikely sources as Thomas Jefferson, Chief Justice John Marshall, professors Leslie Wolf-Phillips and John Agresto, and the Argentine Supreme Court, he pronounced that the court remained independent and the guardian of the Constitution, retaining the role as 'the beneficial expression of a laudable political realism' so as to 'attempt to save all the institutional values that remained to be saved'. What did this mean? In effect, the 800-page judgment meant only one thing: the military takeover and the suspension of the Constitution were valid.[33]

Gold-crested volumes of his own judgment were distributed by Chief Justice Khan himself at each of the numerous conferences he attended after the pronouncement. In his speeches he highlighted how his judgment, as 'the beneficial expression of a laudable political realism,' had saved 'all the institutional values that remained to be saved.'

Unlike the Begum Nusrat Bhutto case (1977), the Zafar Ali Shah judgment (2000) did not even pay adequate lip service to the principles enshrined in the Jilani case. What 'institutional values' the court was purporting to save remains a mystery and would perhaps be known only to the judges. None was specifically identified or spelt out.

The one most important 'institutional value' espoused by the superior judiciary all over the world was, of course, put in extreme jeopardy. Both under General Zia's regime and during General Musharraf's tenure prior to mutated 'restorations' of the Constitution, habeas corpus remained effectively suspended and the superior courts, despite assertions to the contrary, accepted this diminution in judicial authority.

Not that the Constitution was restored by either general in the same original form in which he had suspended it. Zia had been forced to restore the Constitution by a vigorous and popular movement led by the Movement for the Restoration of Democracy (MRD). Musharraf was compelled to do so by the change in the global environment in the wake of the 9/11 tragedy. However, since both Zia and Musharraf had been endowed by the Supreme Court in the Bhutto (1977) and the Shah (2000) judgments with the authority to amend the Constitution, the Constitution, when restored, was certainly not the same document. It was a mutilated version of the Constitution of 1973. The amended and restored Constitution subordinated parliament to the executive. The effect of both judgments was thus to empower the civil and military bureaucracy and enfeeble democratic and political institutions.

the political parties

But it was not as if the political elements displayed any great verve and energy. We have seen how most displayed opportunism and an inherent inability to create, or defend, space for civilian political structures in the early years of Pakistan.

Democracy cannot flourish without political parties. Political parties have, in general, failed Pakistan. The All India Muslim League that led the Pakistan movement was not even a party in the real sense. It was a movement. Upon Independence, it should have been converted into a proper political party with structures and identifiable cadres and office-bearers from the grass roots to the top. But Jinnah kept a more than necessary tight control on it. He nominated the members to every committee and parliamentary board. As K. K. Aziz points out, he also 'gave more attention to winning over established non-League provincial leaders like Sir Sikandar Hayat Khan than to organizing the party at grass roots level.'[34] Jinnah also failed to set up and empower a proper secretariat or central office of the League. And then Jinnah died in September 1948. That left the Muslim League in the lurch and totally at sea.

With the Muslim League, the oldest, as a starting point, we may observe that Pakistan's political parties have generally been of three types: parties with a nationwide constituency, regional parties and religious parties.

However, all parties have shown certain common attributes. K.K. Aziz identifies some of these. The leader exercises the greatest influence and control over the policy and objectives of the party. He is above criticism from within his own party even when he makes serious mistakes. The leader nominates the party's executive committee and other central and provincial office bearers and retains the authority to remove any office holder. 'With the single exception of Zulfiqar Ali Bhutto of (the People's Party) in the years 1967 to 1976 ... strong leadership and a well organized party have never appeared together in Pakistan.'[35] Pakistani political parties have also been afflicted with splittism and factionalism.

The Pakistan Muslim League and the Pakistan People's Party are the only two political parties with considerable nationwide support in the general public. The Pakistan Muslim League has always claimed to be the heir to the founding fathers of Pakistan. It was itself founded in Dhaka in 1906. It came late in the Indus region (that became Pakistan). Most of its early leadership therefore came from India and lacked a political constituency in Pakistan. This leadership was averse to holding a general election and did not do so. Instead they engaged in the merry-go-round of politics until all parties were dissolved by Ayub Khan's martial law administration in 1958. Ayub Khan revived the party in 1962 and usurped the leadership at a convention of pliable and pro-regime Muslim League members. The party split, with those opposed to the government summoning the council of the League and forming the PML (Council) against the PML (Convention). Then Zia banned all political parties in 1977, revived them in 1985 and nominated M. K. Junejo as prime minister. Zia's nominee also became the head of the PML (Zia). Upon his removal as prime minister in May 1988, the Muslim League split again between PML (Zia/Nawaz) led by Nawaz Sharif and PML (Junejo) headed by the ousted prime minister. Other factions that have broken off from the main Pakistan Muslim League on account of personality clashes include PML (Khairuddin), PML (Qasim), PML (Functional/Pagara), PML (Liaqat), PML (Wattoo), PML (Chatha) and PML (Likeminded). The most recent split was when a large number of Nawaz Sharif supporters, headed by Shujaat Hussain, abandoned him upon his ouster by General Musharraf and formed the pro-Musharraf ruling faction, PML (Quaid-e-Azam), often described as the Kings Party. All factions of the party that came together under Nawaz Sharif did, however, share one distinct shift from the original creed of the League. They were united in twice endeavouring to adopt bills that would enforce the Islamic Sharia as the supreme law.

The Pakistan People's Party was formed in November 1967 as a left-of-centre party in the wake of the mass uprising against Ayub Khan's regime. Ayub's former foreign minister, the charismatic Zulfiqar Ali Bhutto, led the new party. The PPP won the majority of the seats in (West) Pakistan in the 1970 elections under a socialist slogan of 'Roti, Kapra Aur Makan' (Food, Clothes and a House). In December 1971, after the separation of East Pakistan, the PPP came into power. Bhutto's rule was personality driven and his socio-economic reforms alienated large numbers of vested interests. The nationalization that he pursued only empowered the bureaucracy while the army made a re-entry into public life as it was called out to put down an insurgency in Baluchistan. In preparation for the 1977 elections Bhutto, somewhat like Jinnah, inducted the traditional landowning families into the party. Many diehard workers felt ignored. When the opposition rejected the electoral results, General Zia imposed martial law and put the resolve of the PPP worker and leadership to the test. Then began the PPP's finest hour. Bhutto preferred to be hanged on a trumped-up charge than to bow to the ruling military junta. His daughter, Benazir, picked up the banner and carried it with grace, dignity, courage and determination through prisons and exile as her workers and colleagues were routinely beaten, jailed, tortured, flogged and even hanged. Zia's death and the elections of 1988 brought the PPP into power. Although the party suffered from splittism and factionalism, Benazir continued to strengthen her hold on it. In 1997, she was elected chairperson-for-life by the senior leadership of the PPP. It remains today the only national liberal party with a strong leadership as well as a countrywide organization and grass roots cadres.

While some small nationalist groups are vigorous in Sindh and Baluchistan, the only significant regional parties are the Awami National Party (ANP) in the North West Frontier Province and the Muttahida Qaumi Movement (MQM) in Karachi and Hyderabad. The former, as the successor to Frontier Gandhi Ghaffar Khan's National Awami Party and Red Shirt Movement, has had a steadfast anti-American and left-of-centre programme, although it has shared alliances with the religious parties and draws its support mainly from the khawaneen (the land-owners) of the province. The MQM was formed in the Zia days as a party to literally fight for the interests of the muhajirs who had migrated from India after Partition. It has had a vigorous militant wing. Both parties are confined to a few districts and are personality-dominated.

The Jama'at-i-Islami (JI), the Jamiat-ul-Ulema-i-Islam (JUI) and the Jamiat-ul-Ulema-i-Pakistan (JUP) are the major religious parties in Pakistan. The JI, founded in 1941 by Abul Ala Maudoodi, reconciled itself to the nation-state concept after the creation of Pakistan and has since been pursuing the goal of creating an Islamic state. This past and this goal are shared by the JUI. The JUP is slightly more flexible but none has been able to expand its constituency in any appreciable manner beyond the narrow sectarian base that it began with. I will be discussing the role of these religious parties at some length later.

The two parties that did have a nationwide constituency had some inherent flaws and elements that hindered their progress and development. Both were dominated by the feudals. Being the very products and creatures of the colonial state, the feudals were easily manipulated and juggled about by the colonial bureaucracy, even after Partition.

the feudals

Almost without exception, Pakistan's feudals in the colonized lands of NWFP, Punjab and Sindh had obtained their landholdings from the colonial regime, mainly for loyal services rendered. Not more than a handful could trace their ancestors' names in land records preceding the British colonization. The colonial bureaucracy, as we have seen, had retained its grip upon the state in all the post-Partition years. And the compact between the feudals and the bureaucracy continued thereafter.

The bureaucracy maintained the land and revenue records. It registered all land transfers, whether by consent or inheritance. It effectively determined the right of collaterals or neighbours to pre-empt sales of land. It regulated the canals and distributed water. It purchased crops on behalf of the state and maintained minimum prices. Its police arm enabled the feudals to keep the peasant under control. In this overall equation, therefore, the bureaucracy played the role of the senior partner and patron. Obviously, in some individual cases, the role may appear to have been otherwise, with a feudal politician patronizing one or more middle-level bureaucrats. But in general, the civil and military bureaucracy as a whole remained dominant and the feudal always the supplicant at the doorstep.

Of course the feudal domain was rich and attractive. A landed estate also implied a secure and stable social status. The feudal moved around with pomp, show and a swagger. He was the envy of all other classes. So through land grants and marriages, the bureaucracy also began, from the early years, to enter the ranks of the feudals. A strong partnership was forged. It also enabled landowners to acquire more holdings at the time of Partition. And, together, both resisted land reforms. As Ian Talbot points out: 'The failure to introduce tenancy and land reforms in the period 1947-49 ensured that West Punjab followed a vastly different socio-economic and political trajectory than its Indian neighbour. Indeed the unsettled conditions in the aftermath of partition enabled landlords to tighten their grip in Pakistani Punjab. They acquired additional land which they either purchased at rock bottom prices from fleeing Hindus and Sikhs or by "unlawfully" possessing state evacuee property. In many areas they also replaced the *banias* as the main source of agricultural credit.'[36]

The failure, indeed the refusal, of the ruling elite to introduce meaningful land reforms was one of the most debilitating factors in the progress and development of the political system in Pakistan. There was, and is, an obvious injustice and disequilibrium in land holdings in Pakistan. Despite three inadequate attempts at land reforms (in 1959, 1972 and 1977), almost 30 per cent of the total farm area continues to be owned by large landowners, with holdings of 150 acres and above. Many also have concealed and 'benami' holdings far in excess of the maximum holdings permitted by the 1977 Land Reforms Act. The fatal flaw in each of the three land reforms was the same. The class that was required to implement these reforms was also the class that would be most affected by it. Influential landowners, in concert with the subordinate land-records bureaucracy, ostensibly transferred their excess holdings to the names of servants and serfs but retained full control through coercion and powers of attorney. Then a reverse process began in 1990. The Shariat Appellate Bench of the Supreme Court declared that prescription of limits on property holdings was contrary to Islam, and the Land Reforms Act was therefore contrary to the Constitution as it stood after the incorporation of Zia's retrogressive amendments.

The initial failure and the subsequent subversion of the land reforms process kept land, perhaps the most valuable resource in a pre-industrial society, locked in the pre-industrial land tenure system. Regulations also prohibited the use of agricultural land as collateral and security for obtaining industrial and business credit. Economic development thus remained largely frozen. Land reforms would have brought land into the market economy, thus emulating the economic and political success of East Asia and even some countries of Latin America. Soon the farmer in Indian Punjab, having benefited from land reforms in the early years after Partition, was harvesting far more produce from each crop and variety than his counterpart in the Pakistani part of the same erstwhile province. Without land reforms, Pakistan remained locked in a virtual political and economic paralysis. Even capital formation was impeded, slowing down the emergence of a business and industrial elite or a large middle class.

industrial and business classes

The industrial elite and the business classes together were another element of the political economy of Pakistan. Their growth in (West) Pakistan was also, unfortunately, entirely state-sponsored and the gift of the bureaucratic elite. The bourgeoisie thus never became a force seeking the dismantling of the colonial state and its replacement by a democratic structure.

The first blow that a potential process of bourgeois formation suffered was soon after Partition. This took the shape of the migration of all non-Muslim businesses and merchants to India. This left a large void which could not be filled easily or at once. In the rural areas, the void was partially filled by the landowners who themselves assumed the role of money lending. This increased substantially their strength and hold over the peasant. In the urban areas, there was a scramble to occupy shops and business premises evacuated by Sikh and Hindu businessmen. This degraded the moral fibre of a large section of the society.

Few large business families opted for Pakistan. The most prominent amongst those that did, the Habibs, the Adamjis and Ispahanis, set up businesses from scratch and did well in banking, tea, jute and textiles. But the culture of prudent capitalism that these well-established families might have created and disseminated was vitiated by a new breed of rich capitalists.

Pakistan, we have seen, had started with only one textile and one sugar mill in 1947. Fortunately, in the very initial years the Korean War (1949) put a great premium on Pakistan's raw cotton. It raked in a large surplus in foreign exchange. And as the Korean War boom tapered off, the government adopted a policy of fast-track industrialization. It was designed to convert the gains of mercantile capital into industrial capital. To encourage and facilitate the establishment of industries, prospective sponsors were offered project finance on the softest terms. They were also guaranteed protection from competition by tariff barriers against imports. Some began, indeed, to enjoy monopolistic conditions.

At the same time, the state also ensured control over the prices of raw materials such as raw cotton, jute and sugar. The entire process of industrialization and credit was regulated by a system of licences and permits. This ensured both the bureaucrats' control as well as the arbitrariness of a patron-client relationship. Neither self-generated financial resources nor technical professionalism was required to set up any industry. All that was necessary was for the prospective entrepreneur to have good connections with a high functionary of the state, enabling him to obtain the relevant licence. With it would come credit as well as the facility of employing the bureaucratic machinery to acquire land at less than one-fifth of its market value. With the licence would also come the opportunity to obtain foreign exchange from the State Bank. Much of the sanctioned foreign exchange was, in fact, stashed away in foreign accounts by overvaluing imported machinery and other components. Since this accumulation of capital and wealth was only possible under state patronage and had not been earned by sweat and toil, or come from personal or family savings, the industrial elite were nothing more than minions of the bureaucratic state. Credit was doled out. Collaterals were overvalued. Default was rampant. Foreclosure was unheard of. Rescheduling and write-offs were the rule. Tax evasion was widespread. Giants of Pakistani industry had therefore feet of clay. They have never supported the democratic movement or any call for the restoration of democracy.

As the cavalier capitalist flourished, the state became impoverished and differences in incomes and lifestyles became stark. Extremes of prosperity and poverty provided ground for another player to step on to the stage.

the fundamentalists

Jinnah abhorred theocracy. He had spoken often, and unambiguously, about state and religion being separate. As early as 1927, he had supported the Child Marriages Restraint Bill piloted by Rai Haridas Sarda. The bill proposed the adoption of a minimum age for contracting marriages, providing penalties for guardians who gave their minor wards in marriage. The bill was opposed by all the leading Muslim fundamentalists of the subcontinent and even by the Muslim members of the legislative assembly. Nawab Sir Sahibzada Abdul Qayyum from NWFP, A.H. Ghuznavi from Dhaka, M. Yamin Khan from UP and Moulvi M. Shafi Daudi from Bihar were vocal in their opposition, as it was perceived as impinging upon a fundamental parental right allowed by Islam to give the child away in marriage. Jinnah was undeterred and unrelenting. Passionately he stood his ground:

> And if we are going to allow ourselves to be influenced by the public opinion that can be created in the name of religion, when we know that religion has nothing whatsoever to do with the matter – I think we must have the courage to say: "No, we are not going to be frightened by that."

On the eve of Independence in August 1947, Jinnah addressed Pakistan's Constituent Assembly. This was the forum enjoined to draw up the Constitution of the newly created state. The Founding Father's own words at this critical time to this forum can only be the most cogent declaration of Jinnah's thoughts. His words rang loud and clear:

> Therefore, we must learn a lesson from this. You are free; you are free to go to your temples. You are free to go to your mosques or to any other places of worship in this State of Pakistan. You may belong to any religion or caste or creed. That has nothing to do with the business of the State ... Now, I think we should keep that in front of us as our ideal and you will find that

in course of time Hindus would cease to be Hindus and Muslims would cease to be Muslims, not in the religious sense, because that is the personal faith of each individual, but in the political sense as citizens of the State.

But Jinnah died early. The fundamentalists, who had opposed him and his idea of Pakistan, began to regroup and reorganize. In 1949, their influence was mildly reflected in the Objectives Resolution adopted by the Constituent Assembly to provide guidelines for the future Constitution. But the fundamentalists had their field day in 1953 in the anti-Ahmadi riots referred to earlier. How sharply opposed these religious divines were to Jinnah's concept of Pakistan became known to the two judges, Muhammad Munir and M. R. Kayani, who were appointed to inquire into the causes of the riots. The judges noted the importance of Jinnah's August 1947 speech to the Constituent Assembly in words that are most apt:

> The Quaid-i-Azam was the founder of Pakistan and the occasion on which he thus spoke was the first landmark in the history of Pakistan. The speech was intended both for his own people, including non-Muslims, and the world, and its object was to define as clearly as possible the ideal to the attainment of which the new State was to devote all its energies. There are repeated references in this speech to the bitterness of the past and an appeal to forget and change the past and to bury the hatchet. The future subject of the State is to be a citizen with equal rights, privileges and obligations, irrespective of colour, caste, creed or community. The word "nation" is used more than once and religion is stated to have nothing to do with business of the State and to be merely a matter of personal faith for the individual.

The judges then turned to the ulema, read out Jinnah's speech to them and asked their opinion:

> We asked the *ulema* whether this conception of a State was acceptable to them and everyone of them replied in an unhesitating negative, including

the Ahrar and erstwhile Congressites, with whom before the Partition this conception was almost a part of their faith. If Maulana Amin Ahsan Islahi's evidence correctly represents the view of Jama'at-i-Islami, a State based on this idea is the creature of the devil, and he is confirmed in this by several writings of his chief, Maulana Abul Ala Maudoodi, the founder of the Jama'at. None of the ulema can tolerate a state that is based on nationalism and all that it implies; with them *millat* and all that it connotes can alone be the determining factor in State activity.

The anti-Ahmadi movement did not enlarge the narrow vote bank of the fundamentalists. It did, however, bequeath to the orthodox some clout in the politics of the country at a time when Pakistan was joining US-sponsored military pacts against communism (the Central Treaty Organization and the South East Asia Treaty Organization). The US then was itself in the throes of McCarthyism. The mullahs supported the Pakistani state in its own 'witch-hunt' for intellectuals, writers, free-thinkers, socialists and communists. The campaign made Pakistan into what Ayesha Jalal calls an 'intellectual wasteland'[37]. Writers like Ismat Chughtai and Sajjad Zahir were driven away. Others like Sadat Hassan Manto starved. Yet others like Faiz Ahmad Faiz, Habib Jalib, Sibt-e-Hassan and Major Muhammad Ishaq spent long years in jail.

But the fundamentalists could never yet dream of coming into power. Their honeymoon with a fundamentalist McCarthyist state came to an end when General Ayub took power and promulgated liberal legislation reinterpreting the Islamic family and inheritance laws. And they also continued to be routed in every electoral contest.

Then the fundamentalists found an ally in General Zia-ul-Haq. They sat in his cabinet as he hanged the deposed prime minister, Zulfiqar Ali Bhutto. The Afghan resistance to Soviet occupation was lubricated by US dollars and weapon systems. Pakistani fundamentalist parties fed the ranks of the mujahideen and took full credit for the ouster of the Soviet troops from Afghanistan. In later years, they also rejoiced in the establishment of the Taliban regime.

But even the collapse of the Soviet Union did not substantially increase the vote bank of the religious parties. They were marginalized in the elections held in 1988, 1990, 1993 and 1997. However, October 2002 was somewhat different. The fundamentalists scored well in all areas bordering Afghanistan. The primary reason for that was the intense American bombing a short distance away in Afghanistan. An outspoken anti-American stance is now, for the first time, creating for Islamic religious parties a noticeable constituency. In structure, and by ideology, the religious parties, however, remain opposed to liberal democracy. In most of the areas from which they are returned, women are not allowed to vote. These parties run fundamentalist educational institutions, known as madrassas. These impart a rigid and narrow field of study. In their own party structures, they have both disfranchised and enfranchised cadres. They are thus comfortable with praetorianism. Having supported generals Yahya and Zia, they bailed out General Musharraf in his most difficult hour by voting in favour of his 17th amendment in December 2003. The amendment gave blanket validation to each and every action of the general since the takeover of 12 October 1999. It even permitted General Musharraf to combine the two offices of president and chief of army staff in his own person.

Despite the electoral bonus of anti-American sentiment, were the religious parties also facilitated in obtaining a sizeable presence in Parliament in 2003 by the military regime's anti-democratic electoral management? That is a question that continues to be raised.

electoral management

The military regime was utterly surprised by the result of the first general elections held in Pakistan in 1970, which were also, perhaps, the only entirely free and fair elections to date. The regime had projected a hung parliament without any decisive victor. All projections made by the regime and its managers predicted almost evenly distributed seats among the contesting parties. The final result was completely unexpected. Religious elements and pro-regime factions of the Muslim League were routed. The Awami League led by Sheikh Mujib-ur-Rahman and the PPP headed by Zulfiqar Ali Bhutto swept the polls in East and West Pakistan respectively. Thereafter the army's management skills short-circuited. The rest is history and the making of Bangladesh.

After this, the civil and military bureaucracy decided that it would never be caught on the wrong foot by unforeseen electoral results. Consequent upon the fall of Dhaka and the surrender of the Pakistan Army, military commanders were obliged to defer to Bhutto. But they bided their chance. After two apprehended or actually attempted military coups d' etat, one in 1972 (General Gul Hassan and Air Marshal Rahim Khan) and the other in 1974 (Brigadiers F. B. Ali and Alim Afridi), the army saw its opening after Bhutto's Pakistan People's Party swept the March 1977 polls. The results were rejected by the opposition. Martial law was proclaimed by General Zia-ul-Haq on 5 July 1977.

Zia had an overarching problem: legitimacy. The only legitimate process was a fresh general election. But Bhutto, the prisoner in the death cell, was too popular. Elections had to be avoided. Even the promised elections were postponed. Other sources of legitimacy had to be found. Zia obtained a first respite when the Supreme Court itself deviated from its earlier pronouncement and legitimized him in the Nusrat Bhutto case (1977). Zia then inducted into the government political elements of Bhutto's opposition including the Jama'at-i-Islami. These elements remained in the cabinet until 1979 when they endorsed the decision to execute Bhutto. Zia then embarked upon an aggressive process to 'Islamize' the

Constitution and the laws, seeking to use Islam to provide him legitimacy. But without an electoral process, Zia could not obtain authentic legitimacy in the eyes of the world. And pressure was mounted, as we have seen, by the Movement for the Restoration of Democracy (MRD). Zia was forced to hold an election in 1985. But he played the electoral card with great reserve and caution. He announced general elections but decreed that political parties would not be qualified to participate in them.

The 1985 'partyless elections' brought into being an assembly totally subservient to the military establishment. However, when Mohammad Khan Junejo, the prime minister nominated by Zia himself, began to display some autonomy by signing the Geneva Accord in February 1988 on the Soviet withdrawal from Afghanistan and by ordering an inquiry into a blast in a military ammunition dump in Rawalpindi, Zia invoked his powers under the amended Constitution to dismiss Junejo and to dissolve the assembly. Elections were called for November 1988.

This time the Supreme Court, on a petition by the Pakistan People's Party's chairperson, Benazir Bhutto, ruled that partyless elections were *contrary to* the Constitution. Meantime, Zia died in a plain crash on 17 August 1988. The loss of the army chief-cum-president with an electoral process in full swing put the military establishment in a spin. A PPP victory was clearly written on the horizon but that is what the military establishment wished desperately to avoid. It set about putting together a coalition of anti-PPP political parties called the Islami Jamhuri Ittehad (IJI). To this day, the issue of the alleged distribution of Rs 140 million among some IJI leaders on the orders of the then army chief remains pending before the courts.

The military succeeded in its purpose. No party obtained an absolute majority in the 1988 elections. The PPP was able to form the government with Benazir Bhutto as prime minister only after it mustered the support of some smaller parties and independent members. Since these elements remained under the influence of the civil and military bureaucracy, represented together by acting President Ishaq Khan and Army Chief Aslam Beg, the PPP was required to vote for Khan in his bid for the office vacated by Zia's death and to take his nominees as foreign minister and advisor finance.

In her twenty months in government as prime minister, Bhutto was consistently opposed in all her significant plans, from the release of political prisoners detained by Zia's military regime to her decision to induct the Pakistan Army under civilian control in Sindh to address the breakdown of law and order in that province. The prime minister was allowed no control of the nuclear programme or in shaping the post Soviet-Afghan policy in Pakistan. In fact the ISI, with the approval of the president and the military command, sponsored a mujahideen push towards Jalalabad despite the fact that Bhutto's civilian government opposed it as an ill-conceived design that was destined to fail. When she moved the ISI chief, General Hamid Gul, and appointed her own nominee, a retired general, other elements in the ISI became active in their opposition to her government. Senior operatives were recorded conspiring to overthrow her in a project, code-named 'Midnight Jackals', in October 1989. Finally, when in July 1990 the PPP government in Sindh began a police operation to flush arms out of the strife-stricken city of Hyderabad, units of the Pakistan Army, under direct orders of the chief, blocked the passage of the police, preventing it from getting to the reported arsenal of the insurgents in Pakka Qila in the city. On 6 August 1990, President Ishaq Khan dissolved the National Assembly, dismissing Bhutto's government on charges of corruption. A hostile caretaker administration comprising Bhutto-haters and breakaway elements from the PPP was set up to conduct the ensuing elections. Seven prosecutions were instituted against Bhutto and eleven against her husband. She contested elections running between courts and dates of hearing. Both husband and wife were acquitted of all charges but that was long after the elections were over.

The defeat of the PPP in the 1990 elections was engineered by means of a 'formula' attributed to a senior military officer who was a member of an 'election cell' working directly under the president. The formula entailed a partisan caretaker set-up, prosecutions of the members of the ousted government and 'result reversals' in certain selected constituencies to defeat the ousted party. The formula has been reused with manifest success. The ousted party, howsoever popular, has never won. The dismissal of the Bhutto government in November 1996 by a troika of President Leghari, Army Chief Karamat and Chief Justice Shah was followed by the same pattern: partisan caretakers, prosecutions of members of the ousted party and 'result reversal' in certain selected constituencies without interfering in the polling process on election day in the remaining constituencies.

As the beneficiary of this electoral management in the 1997 election, Nawaz Sharif was expected to play ball and remain subordinate to the president-chief justice-army chief troika. Sharif, however, was no ordinary player. In a stunning and unprecedented 'judicial coup', a ten-member bench of the Supreme Court in Malik Assad's case (1997) ousted the chief justice just as he became openly hostile towards the prime minister. The president, who was supporting the chief justice against the prime minister, resigned. The following year, Sharif obtained Karamat's resignation and, superseding two senior generals, appointed Pervez Musharraf as the new army chief.

In all respects, Nawaz Sharif had already crossed the Rubicon. Inducted as a subordinate player, he had become the dominant power. This could not be countenanced by the civil and military establishment. Thus, when he tried to remove a second army chief in October 1999, he was deposed and arrested along with all the members of his family.

The military takeover of October 1999 was not in sync with the world environment. Unlike the world of 1960s and 70s, there was no other outright military dictatorship except in Burma (Myanmar) which was, appropriately, an international pariah. To Musharraf's good fortune, however, the tragedy of 11 September 2001 changed the world around him. He became a front-line player in the so-called War against Terror. Though not under intense international pressure, he comfortably held general elections in October 2003 under the same formula. Such was the effective use of this 'formula', especially the selectively engineered 'result reversals', that although the PPP (which had to be downsized) obtained the largest number of popular votes cast for a single party (28.42 per cent), it won only 80 seats, while the 'King's Party', the PML-Q, obtained as many as 118 seats with only 26.63 per cent of the total votes cast. A more striking case was that of the Muttahida Majlis-e-Amal, a coalition of religious extremists and also another beneficiary of the 'formula'. It bagged as many as 59 seats with a mere 12.28 per cent of the votes. To further facilitate efforts by the 'King's Party' to garner a majority in the National Assembly, the military regime kept Article 63-A, which penalized party defectors, in a state of 'suspension' even after the Constitution had been restored. As many as 21 PPP members were then induced to defect from their party to enable PML-Q to attain the majority necessary to form a government. The pre- and post-poll manipulations were obvious but much of the world turned a blind eye to the many flaws in the electoral process both before and after the actual voting process. A military regime was once more facilitated, by the international community's studied indifference, in crafting a seeming democratic order. Today, Musharraf, as president and army chief, has such an effective grip over a decisive but pliant majority in Parliament that he has been able to choose, and fire, prime ministers at will. In November 2002, his choice was Zafarullah Jamali. But when Jamali fell from favour, he was forced to resign on 28 June 2004, two days after the assembly had endorsed him by adopting his budget and a day after he had publicly declared that he would not resign. In a meeting with the president the same day he changed his mind. Shujaat Hussain was then inducted for a mere forty days, just enough time to enable the general's third nominee, Shaukat Aziz, to be elected to the National Assembly. He immediately won a vote of confidence upon Hussain's pre-declared resignation. But Musharraf's grip over the pliant majority in Parliament is best illustrated by the quaintly named President To Hold Another Office Act, 2004, passed by Parliament in December 2004 to enable him to simultaneously hold both the offices of president and chief of army staff. Naturally the general continues to call all the shots.

Will the military relinquish or lose its dominant hold on the commanding heights of Pakistan's political system? That does not seem a likely prospect in the immediate future. Even when it does recede further in the background its influence and authority will remain. It is hardly likely to entirely abdicate from its self-proclaimed role of Pakistan's security manager. Even though pressure may increasingly be exerted by emerging and potentially militant movements in the smaller provinces, the army has acquired a great stake in maintaining its political clout even when it is not in power. Furrukh Saleem and Dr Hassan-Askari Rizvi have, in separate articles, established the vast interests that military personnel, as such, have obtained in industry and business, besides the 'military colonization of other institutions'. In a recently submitted written reply to a question raised in the Senate, Pakistan's defence minister informed the House that armed forces welfare bodies had invested in, or were running, as many as 351 industrial and business ventures covering a vast spectrum including cereals, sugar, gas, cement, oil, pharmaceuticals, shoes, textiles, real estate, travel, aviation, agriculture, banking and leasing.[38] With most mainstream political leaders willing to take the 'pragmatic' option of accepting this 'reality' and to work in some sort of arrangement with the military, though that 'arrangement' may differ with parties and leaders, the military will remain a major player in the politics of Pakistan. For the immediate future, therefore, democracy will remain a fellow-traveller at all times, but one travelling on the back seat. But that is bound to change over a relatively longer period.

conclusion

Having come into being through a constitutional, rather than a revolutionary, process, Pakistan had retained the structure of the colonial state from its inception. Lacking an indigenous bourgeoisie, dominated by a feudal elite totally dependent upon the colonial bureaucracy, deprived of well-structured, programme-oriented and duly encadred political parties, and without a judiciary which would jealously protect civil authority and the citizen's rights, Pakistan saw a gradual choking of the democratic spirit from its early days. First, the civil and military bureaucracy and then the fundamentalists filled the vacuum. But the spirit of democracy remains. It burst out in a widespread movement in the late 1960s and then again in the early 1980s, despite the repressive policies of generals Ayub and Zia.

General Zia's was indeed the most regressive and brutal regime that (West) Pakistan has witnessed. He also had the full sanction and support of the religious parties of the country. The brunt of the oppressive military regime was faced by the party of the deposed prime minister, Zulfiqar Ali Bhutto, and the Pakistan People's Party. Military orders and regulations provided for detention without charge or trial, public flogging of political dissidents, military court sentences of imprisonment and death without due process, forfeitures, seizures, house-searches, the complete suspension of *habeas corpus* and pre-censorship of every word put in print by every publication, daily, weekly, monthly or otherwise.

Then, defying the odds, two other communities came to the forefront in resisting Zia's rule: journalists and lawyers. Another inspiring group was women. In February 1982, a group of courageous women, protesting the 'Islamization' of the Evidence Act designed to reduce the value of testimony of a woman to half of that of a man, were brutally beaten by the police in Lahore. The cross-party unity shown by the journalists, lawyers and women gave great impetus to a broad, united and widespread movement: the Movement for the Restoration of Democracy, in which several political parties joined hands to resist martial law. The full might of the military regime was unleashed upon the MRD in spring of 1981 and again in the fall of 1983 but the clarion call for democracy could not be suppressed. Zia had to relent. Elections were called in 1985. These have thereafter been held periodically. And the principle of universal adult suffrage is now a recognized and irreversible principle. This may seem a natural concomitant in most democracies but given Pakistan's experience and history, this is a major achievement in itself. The fact that even military dictators are convinced that full suffrage elections are unavoidable and inevitable is testimony that the spirit of democracy in Pakistan is indeed irrepressible. I believe that one day it must prevail to the fullest extent by wresting complete supremacy and sovereignty.

---

1. For a more detailed study of the author's exposition of the primordial roots of the Indus-India divide see: Aitzaz Ahsan, *The Indus Saga and the Making of Pakistan*, OUP, Karachi 1996.
2. Aitzaz Ahsan, ibid., p. 233.
3. Aitzaz Ahsan, ibid., p.292.

4. Aitzaz Ahsan, ibid., p. 292.
5. V.D. Mahajan, *India Since 1526,* S. Chand and Co. Ltd., New Delhi, Part II pp. 379-80.
6. Aitzaz Ahsan, op cit, p. 293.
7. Although no units of the Indian Army were raised in Baluchistan, a large number of Baluch were taken in regular and irregular levies by local British commanders and administrators, thus opening a means of employment not previously available.
8. M. O'Dwyer, *India as I Knew It:* 1885-1922, (1926) p. 213, quoted in Bahagwan Josh, *Communist Movement in the Punjab,* London.
9. Imran Anwar Ali, 'Business and Power in Pakistan', article in *Power and Civil Society in Pakistan,* edited by Weiss and Gilani, (2003), OUP, Karachi, p. 103.
10. Imran Anwar Ali, ibid., p. 104.
11. Imran Anwar Ali, ibid., p. 104.
12. Imran Anwar Ali quoted by Jean-Luc Racine in the Introduction to *Pakistan: Contours of State and Society* (Edited by Mumtaz, Racine and Ali, (2002) OUP, Karachi, p. xiii.
13. Federation of Pakistan Vs. Moulvi Tamizuddin Khan reported as PLD 1955 Federal Court p. 240.
14. Federal Court's Opinion on the Reference by His Excellency the Governor General reported as PLD 1955 Federal Court, p. 435.
15. Ian Talbot, *Pakistan, A Modern History:* (1999) Vanguard Books, Lahore, p. 126.
16. Altaf Gauhar, *Ayub Khan, Pakistan's First Military Ruler* (1994) Sang-e-Meel, p. 136.
17. Altaf Gauhar, ibid., p. 144.
18. Altaf Gauhar, ibid., p. 125.
19. Hamida Khuhro, *Mohammd Ayub Khuhro, A Life of Courage in Politics,* Ferozesons, 1998, p. 440.
20. Ian Talbot, op cit, pp.145-46
21. Ayub Khan, *Friends Not Masters, A Political Autobiography;* OUP, 1967, Karachi, p. 21.
22. Hamza Alvi: *Authorization and Legitimation of State Power in Pakistan.* See: http://ourworld.compuserve.com/homepages/sangat.powertt.htm.
23. Hamida Khuhro, ibid., p. 409.
24. PLD 1955 FC 240, ibid.
25. Usif Patel Vs. The Crown: reported as PLD 1955 Federal Court, p. 387.
26. PLD 1955 FC 435, ibid.
27. The welfare of the people is the supreme law.
28. PLD 1958 Supreme Court, p. 533.
29. Asma Jilani Vs Government of the Punjab: PLD 1972 Supreme Court, p. 139.
30. Begum Nusrat Bhutto Vs Chief of Army Staff: PLD 1977 Supreme Court, p. 657.
31. In a contempt of court case against him, General Aslam Beg told the Supreme Court on 1 March 1993 that Senate Chairman Wasim Sajjad had carried his message to the Supreme Court on 5 October 1988 to block restoration of the Junejo government. *Dawn,* Karachi, 2 March 1993.
32. Syed Zafar Ali Shah Vs. General Pervez Musharraf: PLD 2000 Supreme Court, p. 869.

33. Syed Zafar Ali Shah Vs. General Pervez Musharraf: PLD 2000 Supreme Court, p. 869.
34. K.K. Aziz: *Pakistan's Political Culture, Essays in Historical and Social Origins,* Vanguard, 2001, p. 70.
35. K.K. Aziz, ibid., p. 78.
36. Ian Talbot, *Pakistan: A Modern History,* Vanguard, 1999, p. 123.
37. Ayesha Jalal, *The State of Martial Rule: The Origins of Pakistan's Political Economy of Defence;* Cambridge, 1985, p. 123.
38. *The NATION* Islamabad, 27 April 2005.